CUT AND CREATE!

BUGS AND OTHER CREATURES

EASY STEP-BY-STEP PROJECTS THAT TEACH SCISSOR SKILLS

Written and illustrated by Kim Rankin

Teaching & Learning Company

1204 Buchanan St., P.O. Box 10
Carthage, IL 62321-0010

This book belongs to

_____

Cover by Kim Rankin

Copyright © 1997, Teaching & Learning Company

ISBN No. 1-57310-082-X

Printing No. 9876543

Teaching & Learning Company
1204 Buchanan St., P.O. Box 10
Carthage, IL 62321-0010

TABLE OF CONTENTS

Dear Teacher or Parent,

"I did it myself" is a phrase which can be the foundation for a lifetime of accomplishment and positive self-esteem.

Cut and Create activities can be used by the teacher or parent to develop a variety of important early skills and to provide projects in which children can take pride and succeed.

- Simple patterns and easy, step-by-step directions develop scissor skills and give practice in visual-motor coordination. The scissor rating system in the upper right-hand corner on the first page of each project quickly identifies the easiest projects (✂), moderate (✂✂) and challenging (✂✂✂).
- Materials used are inexpensive and readily available.
- Finished products are fun, colorful and have myriad uses from play items to props; room decorations for walls, bulletin boards or mobiles; learning center manipulatives for counting, sorting, classifying or labeling; gifts or favors for parties or guests; and much more.

The simple and fun activities included in this book will help young learners build a solid base for a variety of skills such as: following directions, observation, discrimination and information processing. A variety of learning styles is addressed including visual, auditory and tactile.

Your art program, whether structured or serendipitous can benefit from these simple and sequenced scissor skill activities. You students will

- develop manual dexterity
- communicate
- learn to control his or her environment by being responsible for tools and materials
- observe
- discriminate (by color, shape, texture)
- sort, order, group and engage in other math processes
- imagine!

We hope you and your students will enjoy these projects. They have been designed to stimulate learning and creativity in a way that is simple and fun. So go cut and create! And have a good time!

Sincerely,

Kim

Kim Rankin

SHAPES

Shapes are seen and used in everyday life. You can find them on street signs, houses, windows and rooftops. Notice the shape of a box of crackers, the crackers and a plate. Look at books, desks, floor tiles and shelves. The patterns in this book utilize many basic shapes and reinforce familiarity with their forms and names.

Circle is round or the shape of a plate.

Diamond is the shape of a baseball field or kite.

Heart is a popular shape at Valentine's Day.

Octagon is the shape of a stop sign.

Oval is the shape of an egg.

Rectangle is the shape of a door.

Stars may have many points. This star has five points.

Square is the shape of a saltine cracker.

Teardrop is the shape of a raindrop.

Triangle is the shape of a roof on a house.

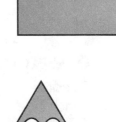

SUGGESTIONS FOR USING SOME OF THE PROJECTS

Different Uses

- Mobiles
- Tabletop or Desk Decorations
- Party Favors
- Take-Homes for Parents
- Refrigerator Magnets (Reduce 25-40%)
- Ceiling Decorations
- Window/Door Decorations
- Greeting Cards (Reduce 30-40%)
- Portfolio Pieces
- Folders (Reduce 30-50%)

Bulletin Boards

Use whatever design you need for the particular season or holiday you will be displaying. You may want to enlarge the patterns for your bulletin board or door.

Mobiles

Here are two suggestions for making a mobile. One way is to use a sturdy paper plate for the top piece. Punch holes around the outer edge of the plate. Use string or yarn in random lengths to attach the ready-made patterns to the top piece.

Another way is the use sturdy tagboard. Cut a rectangle shape approximately 3" x 32" (8 x 56 cm) and staple the ends together to form a circle. Punch holes around the bottom edge. Use string or yarn in random lengths to attach the ready-made patterns. (Note: You will have to reduce the patterns 40 to 50 % so they are not too big for the mobile.)

Greeting Cards

Celebrate a holiday or create an occasion. Handmade greeting cards are a surefire hit for parents, grandparents, relatives and friends. And what better way to say "thank you" to a visitor, custodian, principal, helper, etc.

Materials: *black, gray, red or rust and tan or yellow paper; scissors; glue; black crayon or marker; pipe cleaners*

AMERICAN ROACH

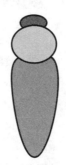

1   Cut one #1 head from red or rust colored paper. Cut one #2 body from yellow or tan colored paper and glue as shown.

2   Cut one #3 tail from gray or black paper and glue to the back side of the body.

3   Cut two #4 wings from red or rust colored paper and glue as shown.

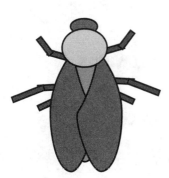

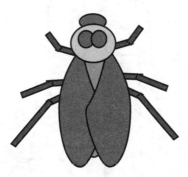

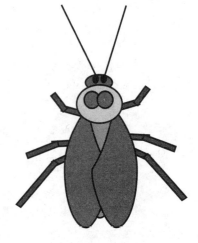

4   Cut eight #6 legs from black paper for the front part of the body and the start of the back legs as shown and glue in place.

5   Cut two #7 legs from black paper to complete the back legs. Cut two #5 circles from red or rust colored paper and glue to the main body as shown.

6   Cut two #8 eyes from black paper and glue on the head, or use a black marker to draw them. Use chenille pipe cleaners for antennas.

Note: If the legs are too difficult for your children to cut out, use black pipe cleaners.

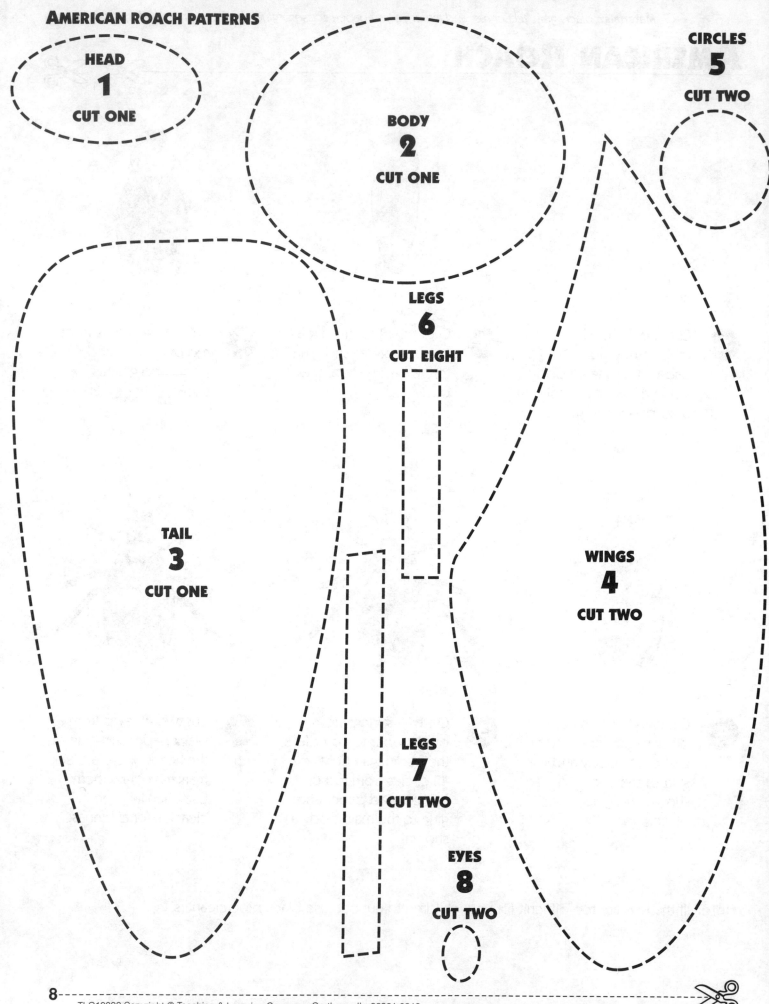

AMERICAN ROACH PATTERNS

HEAD
1
CUT ONE

BODY
2
CUT ONE

CIRCLES
5
CUT TWO

LEGS
6
CUT EIGHT

TAIL
3
CUT ONE

WINGS
4
CUT TWO

LEGS
7
CUT TWO

EYES
8
CUT TWO

Materials: *black, red and white paper; scissors; glue; black crayon or marker; pipe cleaners*
Optional Materials: *brads*

ANT

 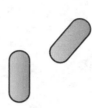 

1 Cut three #1 body and head patterns from red paper. Put two aside. Cut three #2 feet from red paper.

2 Cut six #3 legs from red paper. Glue two of the #3 legs together and glue one #2 to the bottom for the foot. This will form the completed leg. Make three legs.

3 Glue finished legs to the body as shown. (Note: You could use brads to attach legs to the body so they are moveable.)

 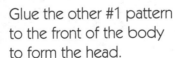

4 Glue one #1 pattern to the back side of the body as shown.

5 Glue the other #1 pattern to the front of the body to form the head.

6 Cut one #4 eye from white paper. Glue to the head. Cut one #5 pupil from black paper and glue to the eye. (Note: You could cut the white part of the eye and use a marker to color in the pupil.) Use chenille pipe cleaners for antennas. Draw on a mouth.

Note: Make lots of these and sing "The Ants Go Marching." Add a craft stick to the back to make a stick puppet.

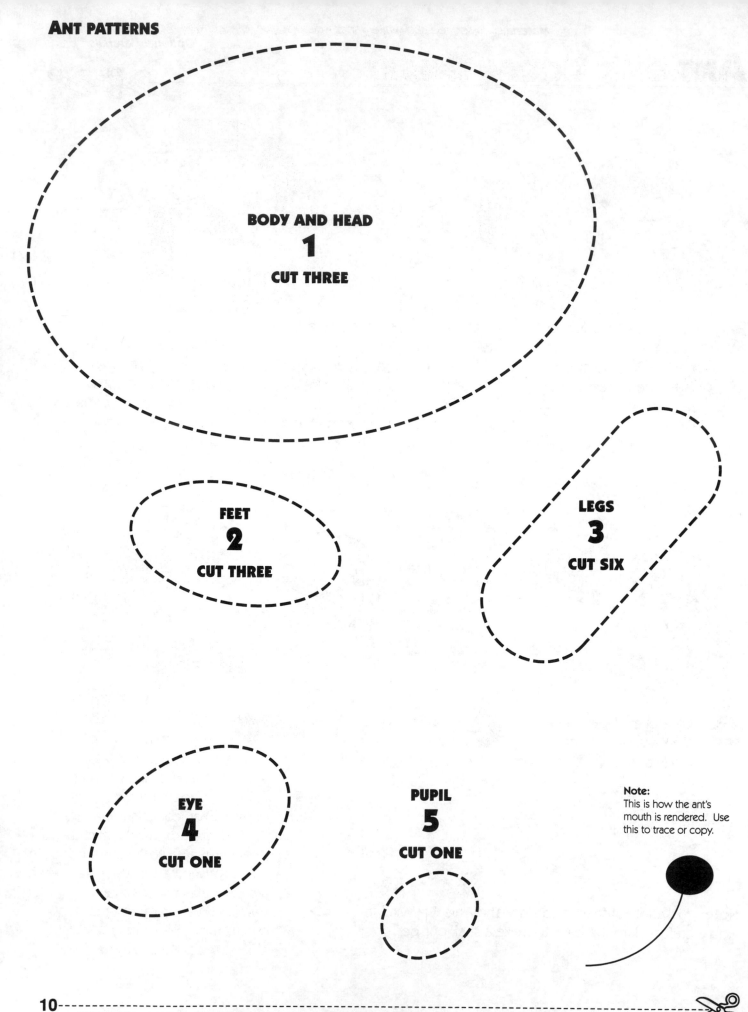

BODY AND HEAD
1
CUT THREE

FEET
2
CUT THREE

LEGS
3
CUT SIX

EYE
4
CUT ONE

PUPIL
5
CUT ONE

Note:
This is how the ant's mouth is rendered. Use this to trace or copy.

Materials: *black, orange, red and white paper; scissors; glue; black crayon or marker*

ARIZONA CORAL SNAKE

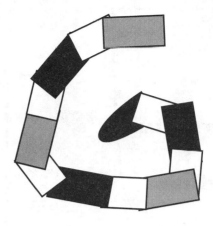

1 Cut two #1 head and tail patterns from black paper. Cut nine #2 body parts from white paper. Cut four #3 body parts from black paper. (This particular snake has white bands on either side of the black.)

2 Cut four #4 body parts from orange paper. In a circular pattern, glue the pieces together. Start gluing at the tail. Remember, use a white piece on either side of the black.

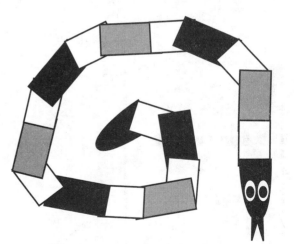

3 You should finish with a white piece. Glue the head to this piece.

4 Cut two #5 eyes from white paper. Glue to the head. Cut two #6 pupils from black paper and glue to the eyes. (Note: You could use a marker to color in the pupils.) Cut two #7 tongue pieces from black paper and glue to the head as shown.

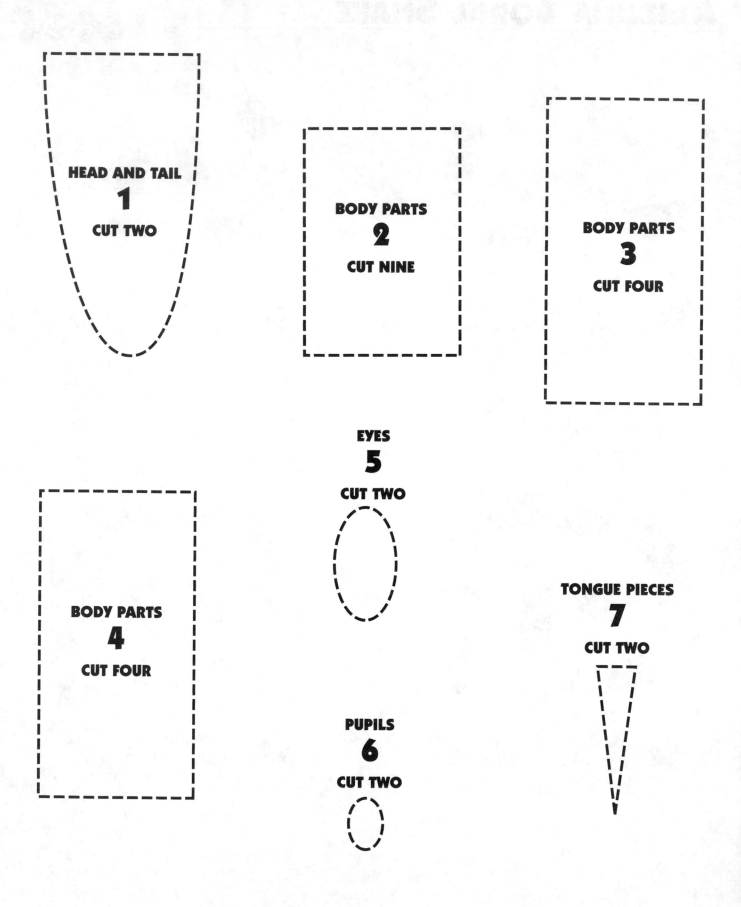

HEAD AND TAIL

1

CUT TWO

BODY PARTS

2

CUT NINE

BODY PARTS

3

CUT FOUR

BODY PARTS

4

CUT FOUR

EYES

5

CUT TWO

PUPILS

6

CUT TWO

TONGUE PIECES

7

CUT TWO

BLACK WIDOW SPIDER

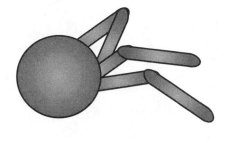

1 Cut one #1 body from black paper.

2 Cut sixteen #2 legs from black paper. Start gluing the legs on the back of the body as shown.

3 Finish gluing the legs to the front side as shown. Cut eight #3 feet from black paper and glue to the ends of the legs.

4 Cut one #4 head from black paper. Glue the head in place as shown. Cut two #5 triangles from red paper for the hourglass shape on the bottom of the body. Glue in place as shown.

5 Spiders have lots of eyes. Cut one #6 eyes from white paper and draw the pupils on with a black marker. Cut two #7 fangs from black paper and glue to the back side of the head.

---13

BLACK WIDOW SPIDER PATTERNS

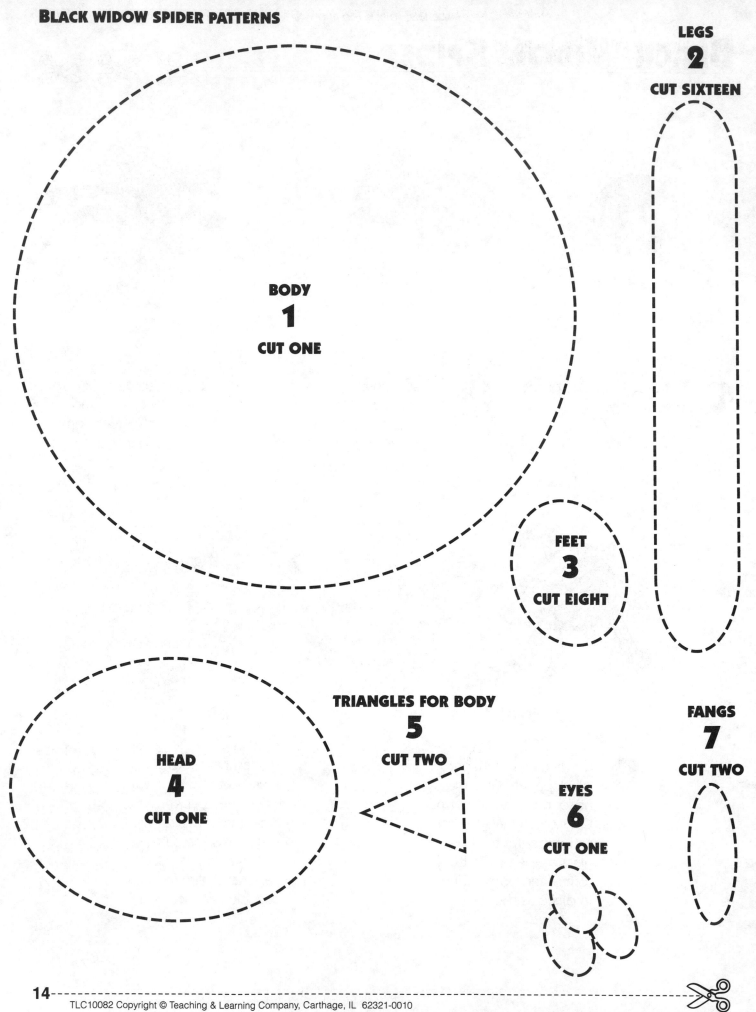

LEGS
2
CUT SIXTEEN

BODY
1
CUT ONE

FEET
3
CUT EIGHT

HEAD
4
CUT ONE

TRIANGLES FOR BODY
5
CUT TWO

FANGS
7
CUT TWO

EYES
6
CUT ONE

Materials: black, gray and yellow paper; scissors; glue; black crayon or marker; pipe cleaners

BLISTER BEETLE

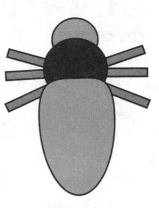

1 Cut one #1 head from gray paper and one #2 body from black paper. Glue these together as shown.

2 Cut one #3 tail from gray paper and glue to the body.

3 Cut six #4 legs from gray or light paper and glue three on each side of the body as shown.

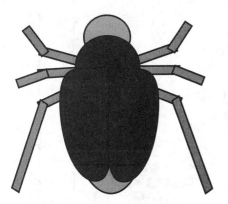

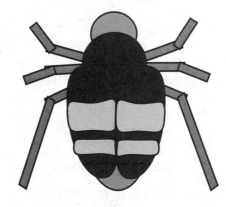

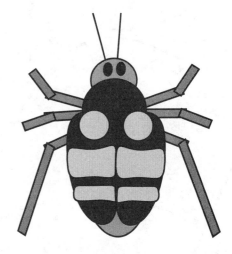

4 Cut four #5 legs from gray or black paper and glue to the front four legs. Cut two #6 legs from gray or black paper and glue to the back two legs. Cut two #7 wings from black paper and glue as shown.

5 Cut two #8 bands and two #9 bands from yellow paper and glue to the wings as shown.

6 Cut two #10 circles from yellow paper and glue to the wings. Cut two #11 eyes from black paper. Glue on the head. Use chenille pipe cleaners for antennas.

BLISTER BEETLE PATTERNS

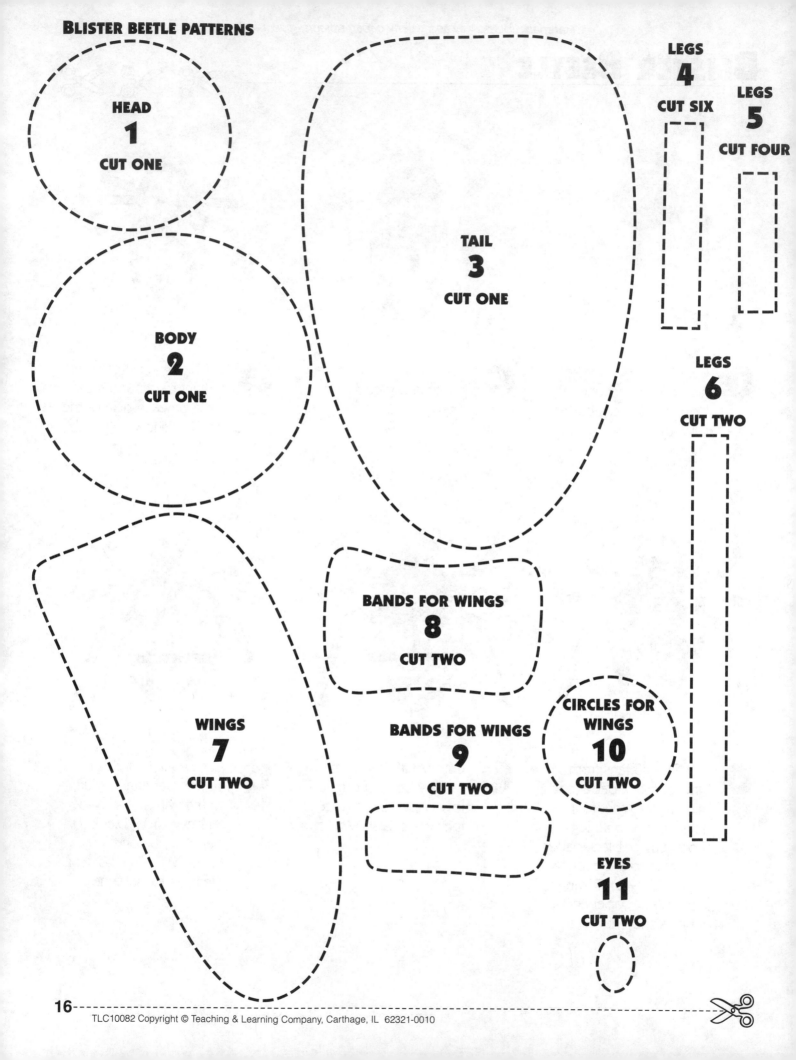

HEAD
1
CUT ONE

BODY
2
CUT ONE

TAIL
3
CUT ONE

LEGS
4
CUT SIX

LEGS
5
CUT FOUR

LEGS
6
CUT TWO

BANDS FOR WINGS
8
CUT TWO

WINGS
7
CUT TWO

BANDS FOR WINGS
9
CUT TWO

CIRCLES FOR WINGS
10
CUT TWO

EYES
11
CUT TWO

16

Materials: black, light gray or silver and white paper; scissors; glue; black crayon or marker

BRISTLETAIL SILVERFISH

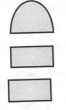

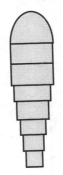

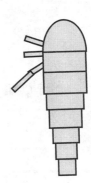

1 Cut one #1 head from silver or light gray paper. Cut one #2 and one #3 body from silver or light gray paper and glue to the head.

2 Cut one each of #4, #5, #6, #7, #8 from silver or light gray paper and glue in that order from large to small.

3 Cut eight #9 legs from silver or light gray paper. Glue three on either side of the body. Add the extra piece to each of the back legs.

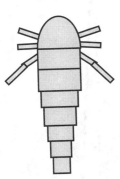

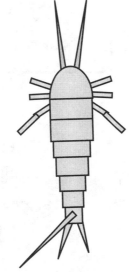

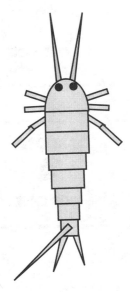

4 This is how your silverfish should look now.

5 Cut two #10 tails from silver or light gray paper and glue as shown. Cut three #11 tail and antennas from silver or light gray paper. Glue one to the back of the silverfish and two to the front of the head for antennas.

6 Cut two #12 eyes from black paper and glue to the head or use a marker to color them.

BRISTLETAIL SILVERFISH PATTERNS

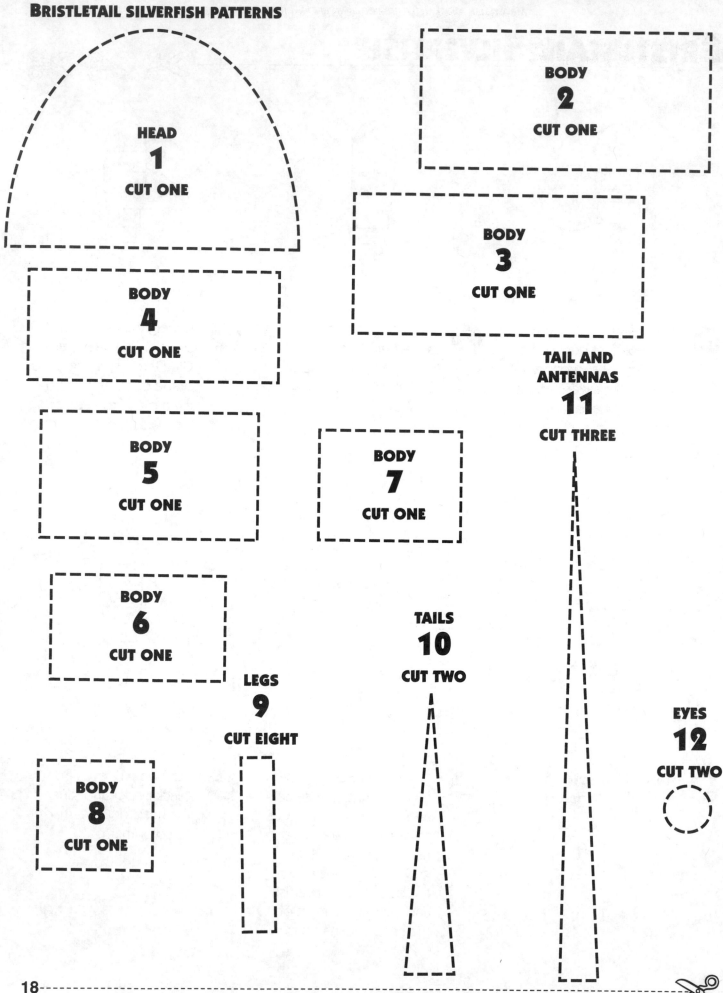

HEAD
1
CUT ONE

BODY
2
CUT ONE

BODY
3
CUT ONE

BODY
4
CUT ONE

BODY
5
CUT ONE

BODY
6
CUT ONE

BODY
7
CUT ONE

TAIL AND
ANTENNAS
11
CUT THREE

TAILS
10
CUT TWO

LEGS
9
CUT EIGHT

EYES
12
CUT TWO

BODY
8
CUT ONE

CATERPILLAR

1 Cut one #1 head from green paper. Cut five #2 body pieces from green paper. Cut one #3 tail piece and one #4 tail piece from green paper.

2 Glue these together from the largest to the smallest as shown.

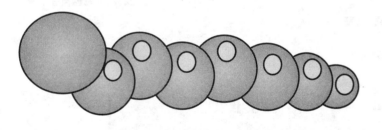

3 Cut one #5 small circle for each body piece and tail piece from light green paper. (Do not cut one for the head.) Glue circles in place as shown.

4 Cut fourteen #6 legs from green paper and glue two to each body piece and tail piece as shown. Cut two #7 eyes from white paper and two #8 pupils from black paper. Glue in place. Cut two #9 antennas from green paper and glue as shown.

CATERPILLAR PATTERNS

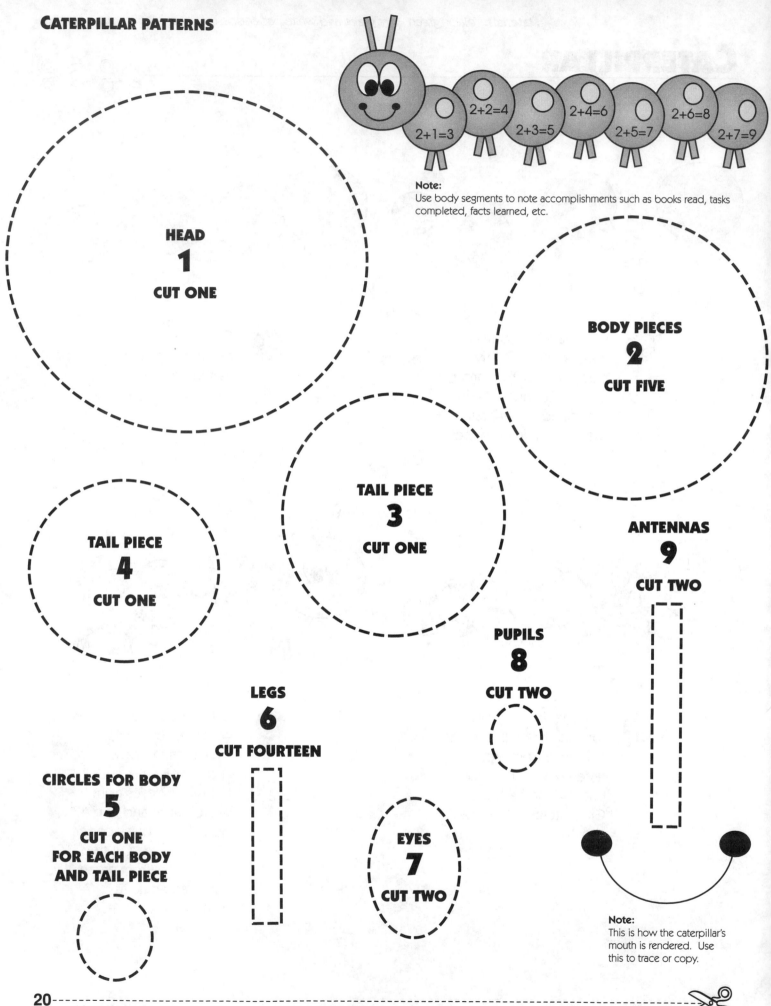

Note:
Use body segments to note accomplishments such as books read, tasks completed, facts learned, etc.

2+1=3
2+2=4
2+3=5
2+4=6
2+5=7
2+6=8
2+7=9

HEAD
1
CUT ONE

BODY PIECES
2
CUT FIVE

TAIL PIECE
3
CUT ONE

TAIL PIECE
4
CUT ONE

ANTENNAS
9
CUT TWO

PUPILS
8
CUT TWO

LEGS
6
CUT FOURTEEN

CIRCLES FOR BODY
5
CUT ONE
FOR EACH BODY
AND TAIL PIECE

EYES
7
CUT TWO

Note:
This is how the caterpillar's mouth is rendered. Use this to trace or copy.

Materials: black, blue, gray and white paper; scissors; glue; black crayon or marker; pipe cleaners

DRAGONFLY

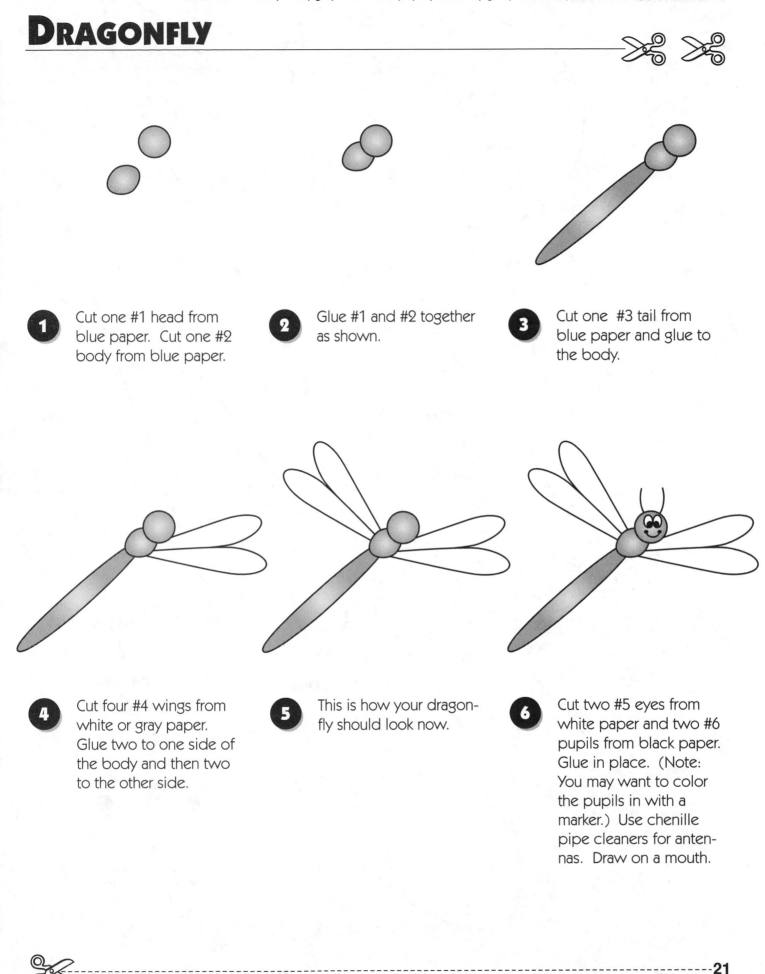

1 Cut one #1 head from blue paper. Cut one #2 body from blue paper.

2 Glue #1 and #2 together as shown.

3 Cut one #3 tail from blue paper and glue to the body.

4 Cut four #4 wings from white or gray paper. Glue two to one side of the body and then two to the other side.

5 This is how your dragonfly should look now.

6 Cut two #5 eyes from white paper and two #6 pupils from black paper. Glue in place. (Note: You may want to color the pupils in with a marker.) Use chenille pipe cleaners for antennas. Draw on a mouth.

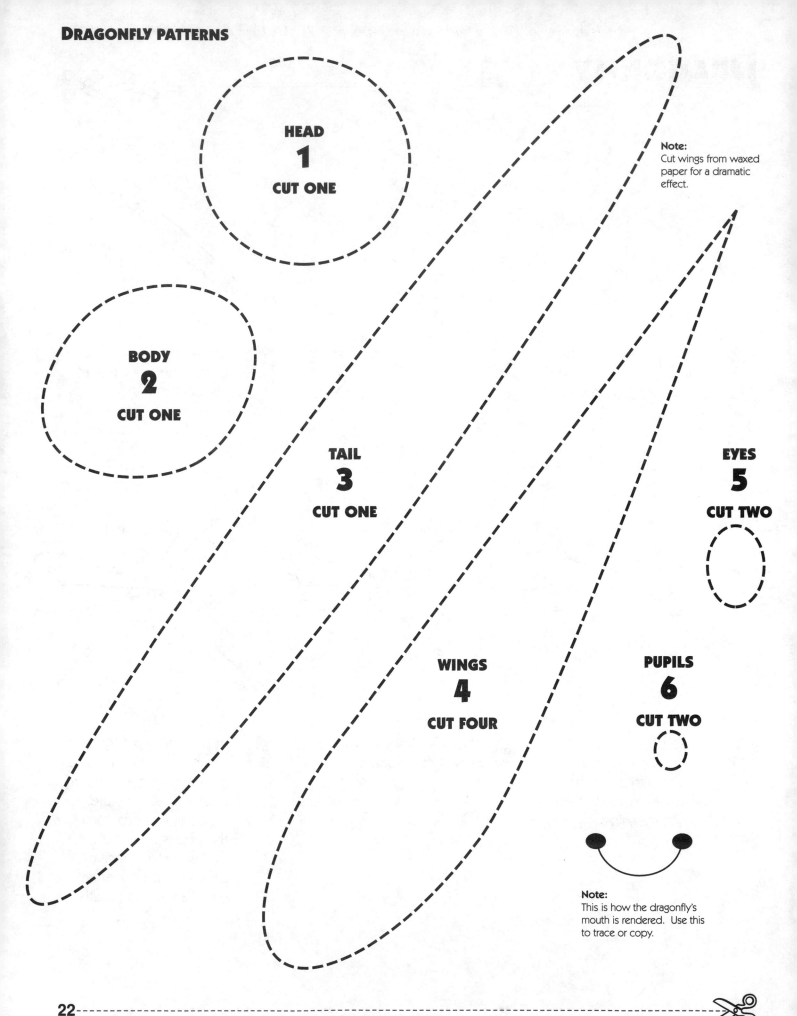

DRAGONFLY PATTERNS

HEAD
1
CUT ONE

BODY
2
CUT ONE

TAIL
3
CUT ONE

WINGS
4
CUT FOUR

EYES
5
CUT TWO

PUPILS
6
CUT TWO

Note:
Cut wings from waxed paper for a dramatic effect.

Note:
This is how the dragonfly's mouth is rendered. Use this to trace or copy.

FIREFLY

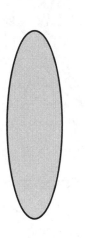

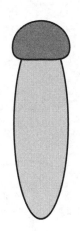

1 Cut one #1 body from yellow paper.

2 Cut one #2 head from orange paper and glue to #1.

3 Cut two #3 wings from black paper. Glue the wings at a slight angle so you can see the yellow body underneath.

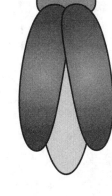

4 Draw on two black eyes with a marker.

5 Use chenille pipe cleaners for antennas.

*Note: If available, neon yellow paper makes a great firefly.

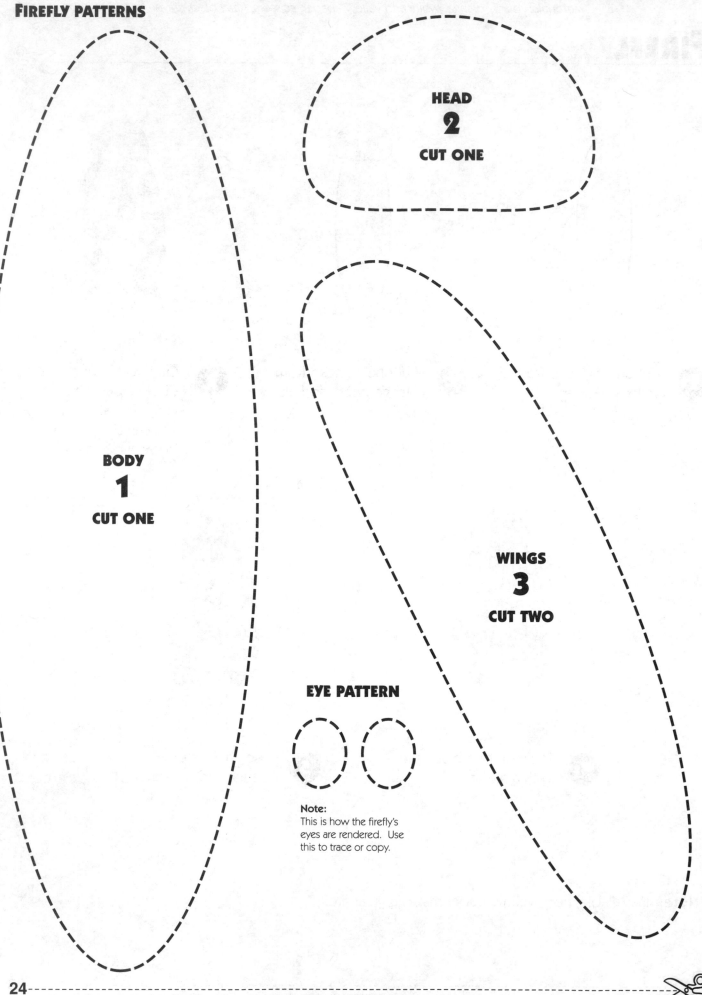

FIREFLY PATTERNS

HEAD
2
CUT ONE

BODY
1
CUT ONE

WINGS
3
CUT TWO

EYE PATTERN

Note:
This is how the firefly's eyes are rendered. Use this to trace or copy.

Materials: *black, green and white paper; scissors; glue; black crayon or marker; pipe cleaners*

GRASSHOPPER

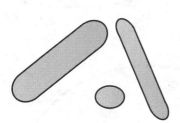 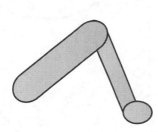 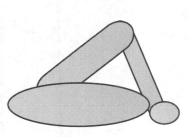

1 Cut two #1 back legs, two #2 back legs and two #3 feet from green paper.

2 Glue these pieces together as shown. Make another just like the first.

3 Cut one #4 body from green paper. Then glue one of the back legs to the back side of the body.

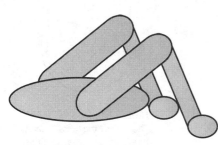 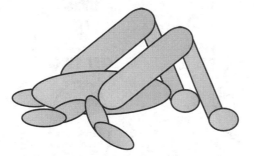 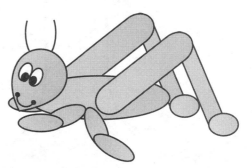

4 Glue the other back legs to the front of the body.

5 Cut five #5 front legs from green paper. Glue one to the back side of the body. Then glue two together to form each of the two front legs.

6 Cut one #6 head from green paper and glue to the body. Cut two #7 eyes from white paper. Glue in place. Use a marker to make pupils. Glue chenille pipe cleaners for antennas.

Note: Use with the Ant on page 9 to dramatize the story, "The Grasshopper and the Ant." Add a craft stick to the back to make a stick puppet.

TLC10082 Copyright © Teaching & Learning Company, Carthage, IL 62321-0010

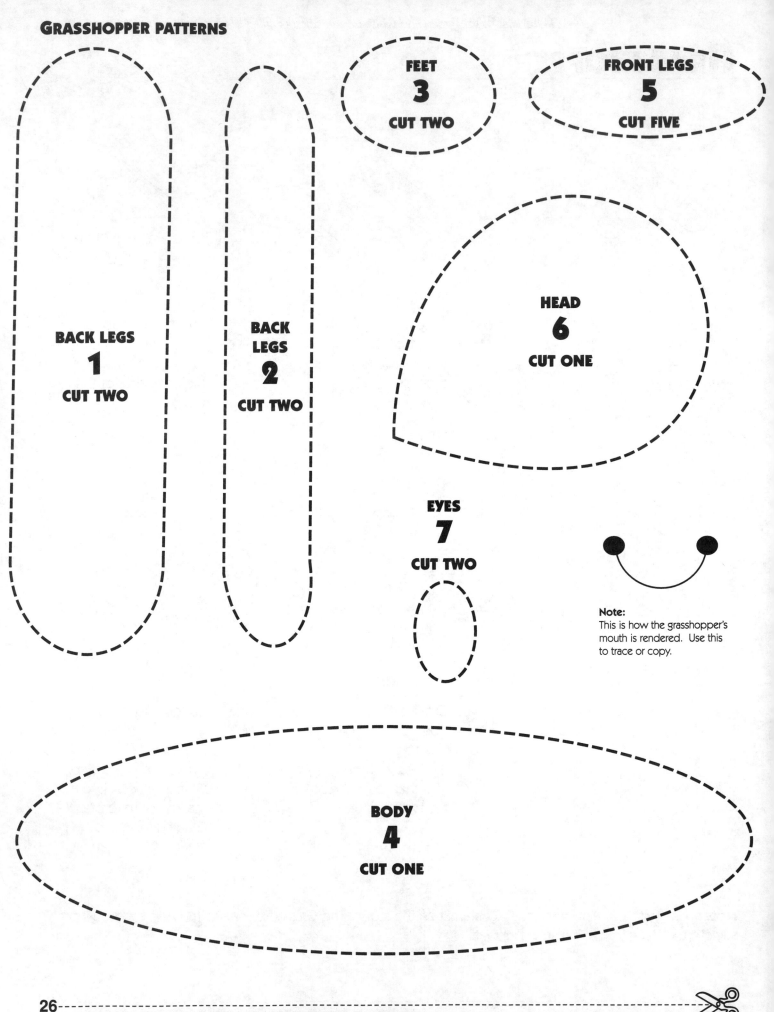

FEET
3
CUT TWO

FRONT LEGS
5
CUT FIVE

BACK LEGS
1
CUT TWO

BACK LEGS
2
CUT TWO

HEAD
6
CUT ONE

EYES
7
CUT TWO

Note:
This is how the grasshopper's mouth is rendered. Use this to trace or copy.

BODY
4
CUT ONE

Materials: black, brown, tan and white paper; scissors; glue; black crayon or marker; pipe cleaners

HONEYBEE

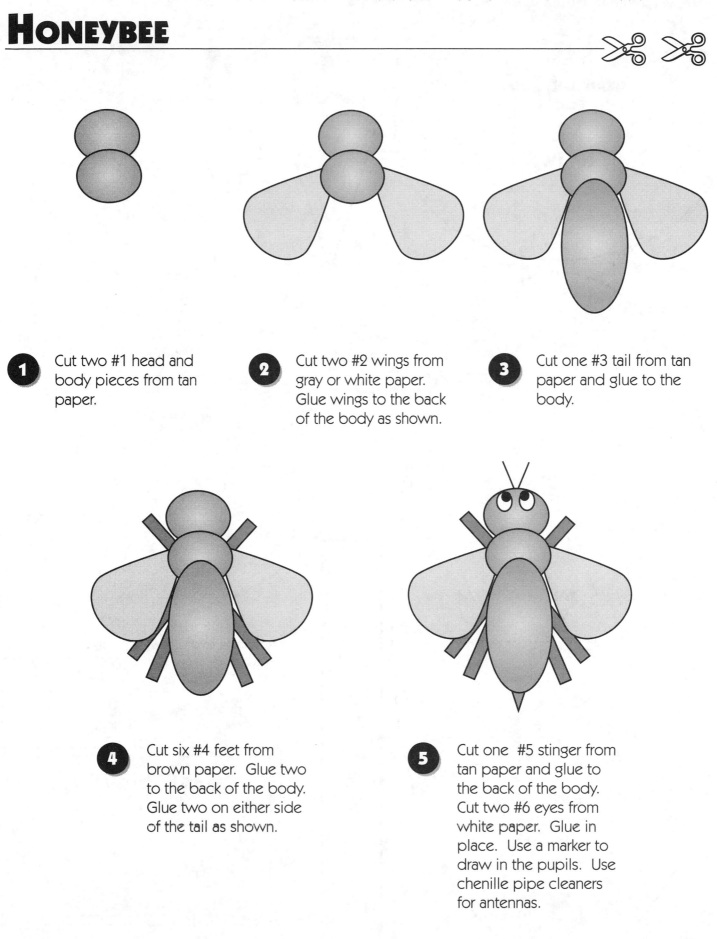

1 Cut two #1 head and body pieces from tan paper.

2 Cut two #2 wings from gray or white paper. Glue wings to the back of the body as shown.

3 Cut one #3 tail from tan paper and glue to the body.

4 Cut six #4 feet from brown paper. Glue two to the back of the body. Glue two on either side of the tail as shown.

5 Cut one #5 stinger from tan paper and glue to the back of the body. Cut two #6 eyes from white paper. Glue in place. Use a marker to draw in the pupils. Use chenille pipe cleaners for antennas.

HONEYBEE PATTERNS

**HEAD AND BODY
PIECES
1
CUT TWO**

**STINGER
5
CUT ONE**

**EYES
6
CUT TWO**

**WINGS
2
CUT TWO**

**TAIL
3
CUT ONE**

**FEET
4
CUT
SIX**

Note: Honeybees are fascinating creatures about which much information is available. Make an interesting, interactive bulletin board with these patterns, showing some of the un"bee"lievable facts your students discover. Place your research questions in a "hive" cut from a brown envelope.

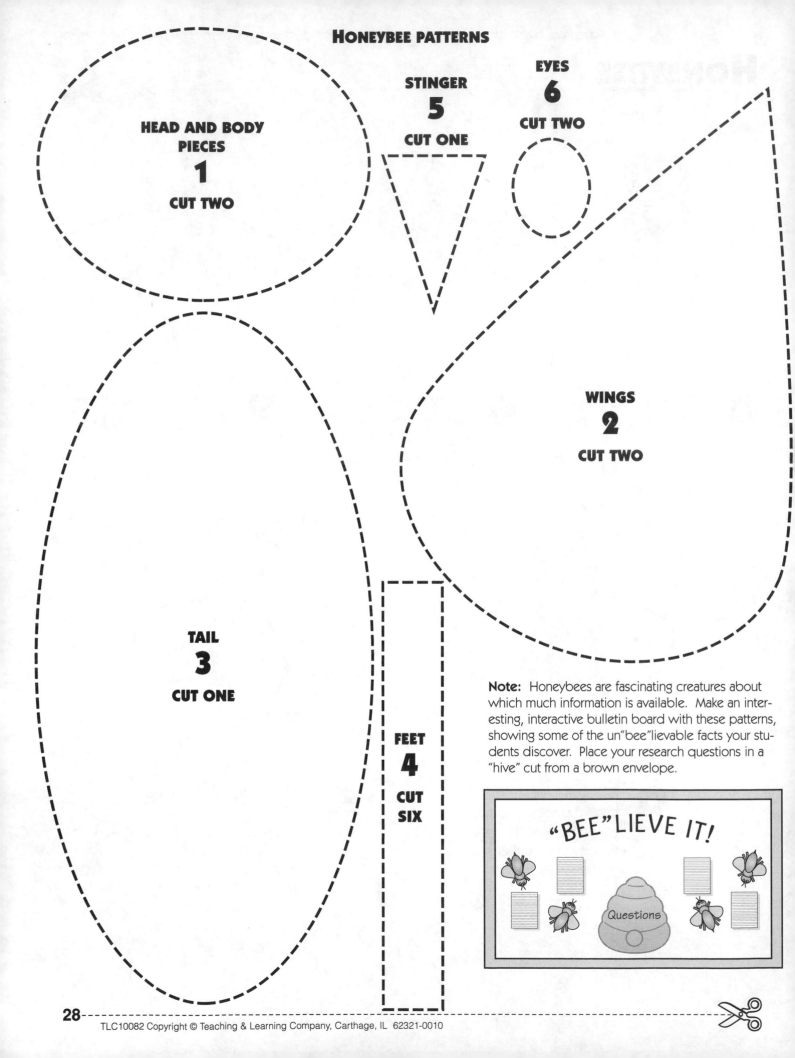

"BEE"LIEVE IT!

Questions

Materials: black, gray and white paper; scissors; glue; black crayon or marker

HOUSEFLY

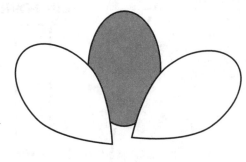

1   Cut one #1 tail from black paper.

2   Cut two #2 wings from white or gray paper and glue to the tail as shown.

3   Cut two #3 head and body pieces from black paper and glue one over the wings. Glue the other over the body as shown, for the head.

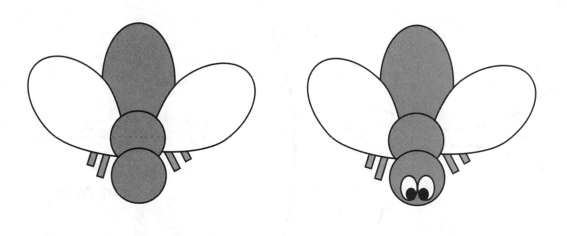

4   Cut four #4 legs from black paper and glue to the back of the wings as shown.

5   Cut two #5 eyes from white paper. Use a marker to color in the pupils.

Note: Use as a prop when singing "Shoo Fly" or "I Know an Old Lady."

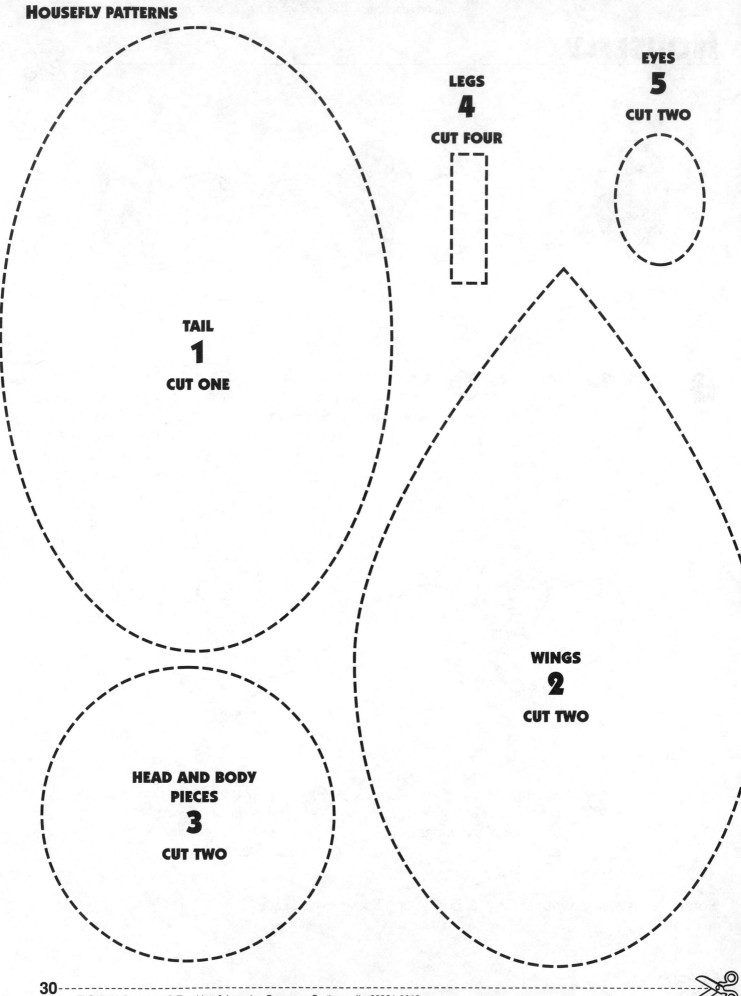

LEGS
4
CUT FOUR

EYES
5
CUT TWO

TAIL
1
CUT ONE

WINGS
2
CUT TWO

HEAD AND BODY
PIECES
3
CUT TWO

Materials: *black, light green and white paper; scissors; glue; black crayon or marker*

INCHWORM

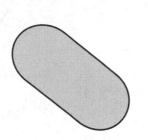 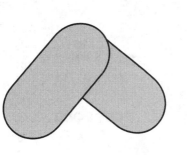 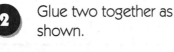

1 Cut four #1 body pieces from light green paper.

2 Glue two together as shown.

3 Add one more as shown. Glue overlapping slightly.

4 Glue the fourth body section as shown. Cut one #2 head from light green paper. Glue in place.

5 Cut two #3 eyes from white paper and two #4 pupils from black paper. Glue in place as shown. Draw on a mouth with black marker.

Note: Do you know the song, "Inchworm," from the movie, *Hans Christian Andersen,* starring Danny Kaye? It's worth the trip to the video store.

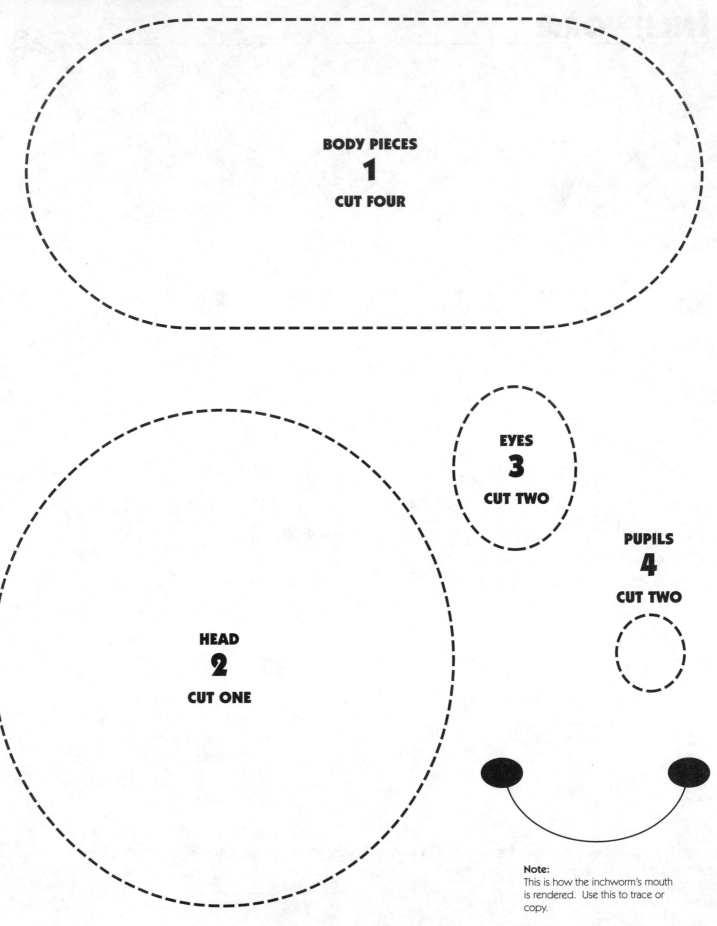

BODY PIECES
1
CUT FOUR

HEAD
2
CUT ONE

EYES
3
CUT TWO

PUPILS
4
CUT TWO

Note:
This is how the inchworm's mouth is rendered. Use this to trace or copy.

LADYBIRD

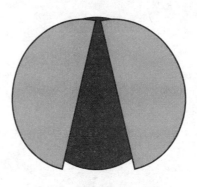

1 Cut one #1 body from black paper.

2 Cut two #2 wings from red paper. Glue the wings on the body at an angle so part of the body shows.

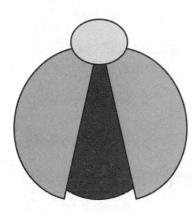

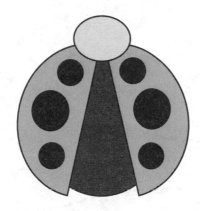

3 Cut one #3 head from gray paper and glue to the top of the body.

4 Cut two #4 large circles from black paper and glue to the middle of the wings. Cut four #5 small circles from black paper and glue to either side of the larger circles as shown.

5 Cut two #6 eyes from white paper. Glue in place. Use a marker to add the pupils. Add chenille pipe cleaners for antennas.

Note: By making the ladybirds in pairs, and varying the number of spots, you can turn these bugs into a matching game.

LADYBIRD PATTERNS

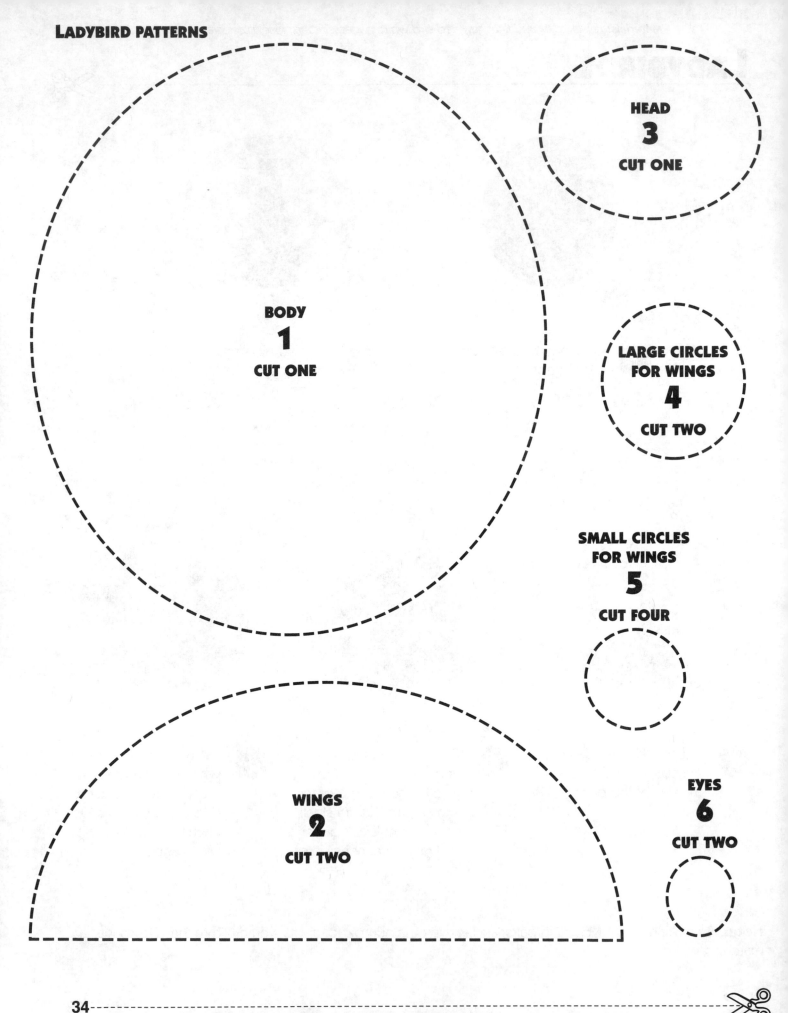

HEAD
3
CUT ONE

BODY
1
CUT ONE

LARGE CIRCLES
FOR WINGS
4
CUT TWO

SMALL CIRCLES
FOR WINGS
5
CUT FOUR

WINGS
2
CUT TWO

EYES
6
CUT TWO

Materials: *tan paper, scissors, glue, black or brown crayon or marker*

LEOPARD LIZARD

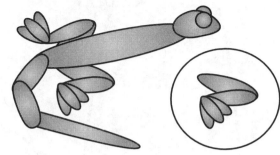

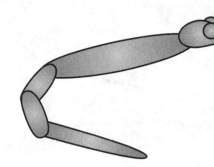

1 Cut one #1 body from tan paper. Cut one #2 head from tan paper. Assemble as shown. Cut two #3 eyes from tan paper and glue to either side of the head as illustrated.

2 Cut two #4 tails and one #5 tail from tan paper. Glue as shown.

3 Cut two #6 back legs, two #7 back legs and six #8 toes, all from tan paper. Assemble the legs as shown in the inset using one #6 for the upper leg, one #7 for the lower leg and three #8s for the toes.

4 Cut one #9 front leg from tan paper and glue to the front of the body. Cut one #10 front paw from tan paper and glue in place as shown.

5 Make lots of leopard spots on the head, body and tail pieces with a black or brown crayon or marker.

6 Draw a pupil on the eye with black crayon or marker.

Note: Give each child an 8½" x 11" (22 x 28 cm) sheet of butcher paper; then splatter paint the paper with black or brown tempera paint. Let dry. Use the spotted paper to cut out the lizard shapes.

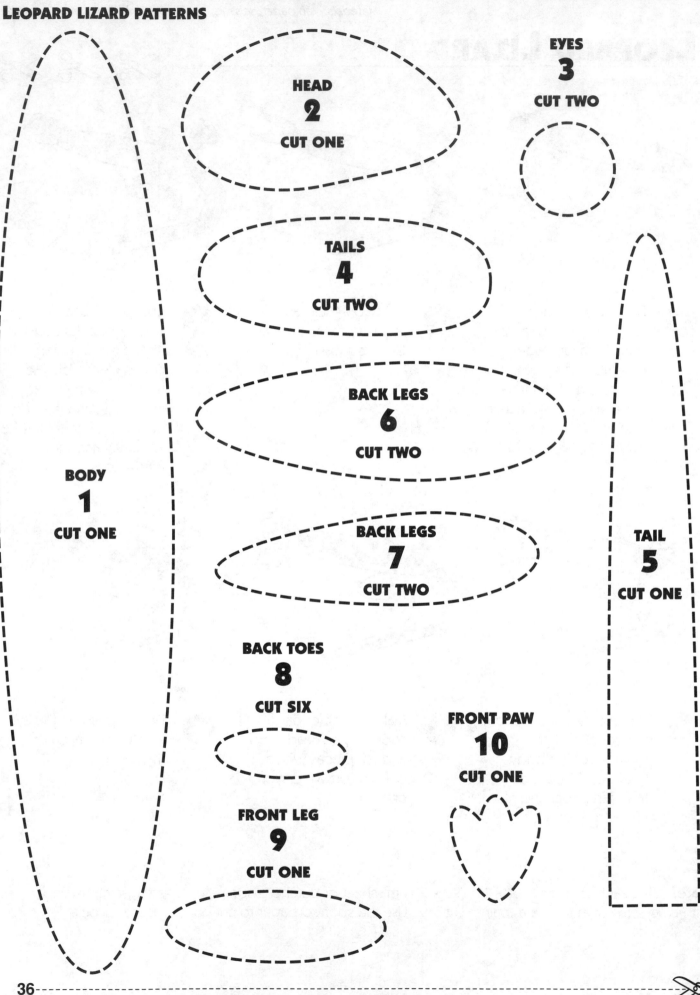

LEOPARD LIZARD PATTERNS

EYES
3
CUT TWO

HEAD
2
CUT ONE

TAILS
4
CUT TWO

BACK LEGS
6
CUT TWO

BODY
1
CUT ONE

BACK LEGS
7
CUT TWO

TAIL
5
CUT ONE

BACK TOES
8
CUT SIX

FRONT PAW
10
CUT ONE

FRONT LEG
9
CUT ONE

Materials: black, orange or reddish-orange and white paper; scissors; glue; black crayon or marker; pipe cleaners

LOBSTER

1 Cut one each of #1, #2, #3 and #4 tail sections from orange or reddish-orange paper.

2 Glue these triangles in the order as shown.

3 Cut two #5 front legs and one #6 head from orange paper. Glue the two legs on either side of the bottom half of the triangle body. Then glue the #6 head in the center as shown.

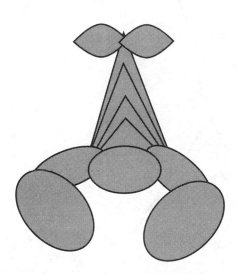

4 Cut two #7 claws from orange paper. Glue one to each #5 leg. Cut two #8 tail fins from orange paper. Glue on either side of tail section #1.

5 Cut two #9 and four #10 from black paper for the claws. Glue these squares at an angle to form claws. Alternate small, large and small squares on each claw as shown.

6 Cut two #11 eyes from white paper. Glue on the head. Use a black marker to color in the pupils. Add chenille pipe cleaners for antennas.

LOBSTER PATTERNS

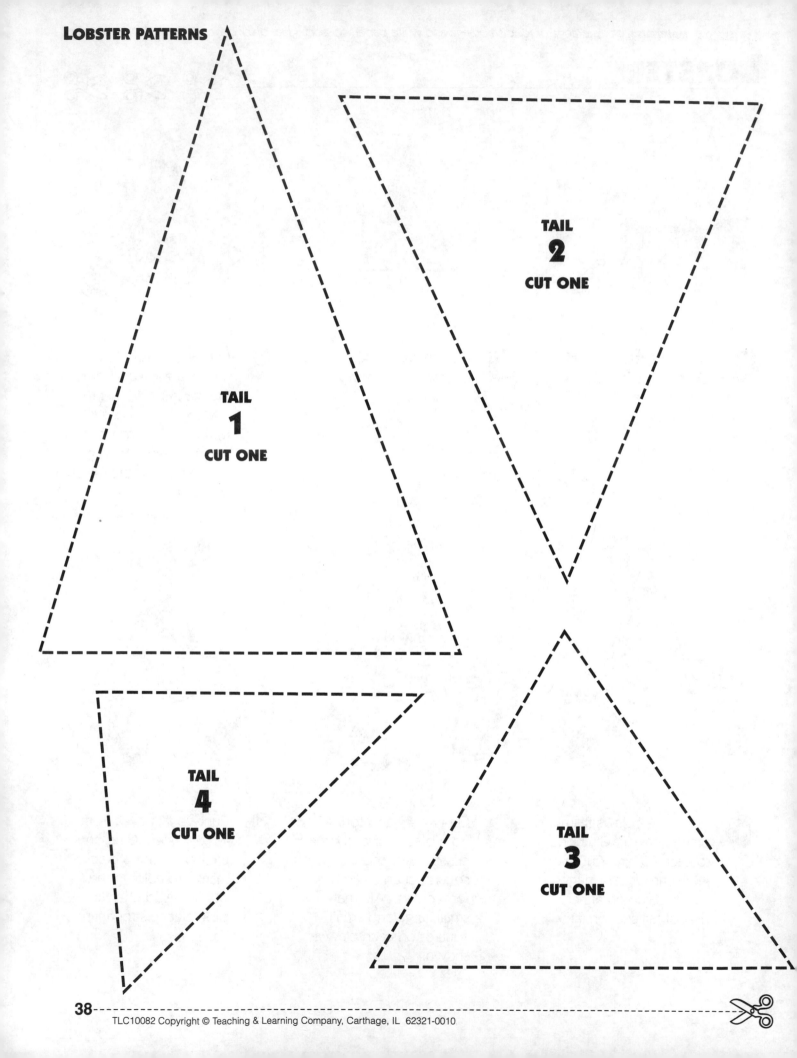

TAIL
2
CUT ONE

TAIL
1
CUT ONE

TAIL
4
CUT ONE

TAIL
3
CUT ONE

LOBSTER PATTERNS

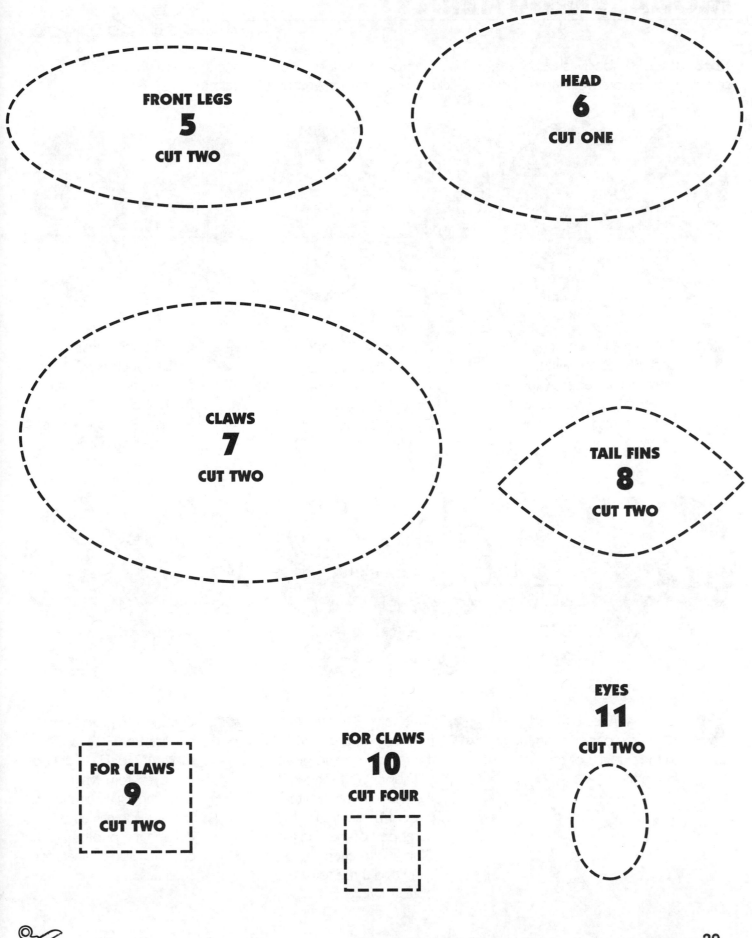

FRONT LEGS
5
CUT TWO

HEAD
6
CUT ONE

CLAWS
7
CUT TWO

TAIL FINS
8
CUT TWO

FOR CLAWS
9
CUT TWO

FOR CLAWS
10
CUT FOUR

EYES
11
CUT TWO

Materials: *black, dark gray, orange and white paper; scissors; glue; black crayon or marker; pipe cleaners*

MONARCH BUTTERFLY

Note: The basic body is easy to assemble. For younger students, or beginners, you might just offer a selection of decorative shapes and let children design their own butterfly patterns.

1 Cut two #1 top wings and #2 bottom wings from black paper. Glue the two wing parts together and overlap as shown.

2 Cut two each of #3, #4, #5 and #6 teardrop shapes from orange paper. These are for the top part of the wings. Glue in place.

3 Cut two #7 teardrop shapes and six #8 ovals from orange paper for the bottom part of the wings. Glue one set to each bottom wing.

4 Cut one #9 body from dark gray paper and glue in the middle of the butterfly.

5 Cut twelve #10 circles from orange paper for the top wings and glue as shown. Cut sixteen #11 circles from white paper. These are for the outer part of the wings. Glue five to each top wing and three to each bottom wing.

6 Cut one #12 head from gray paper. Glue to the top of the body. Cut two #13 eyes from white paper and glue as shown. Use a black marker to color in the pupils. Add chenille pipe cleaners for antennas.

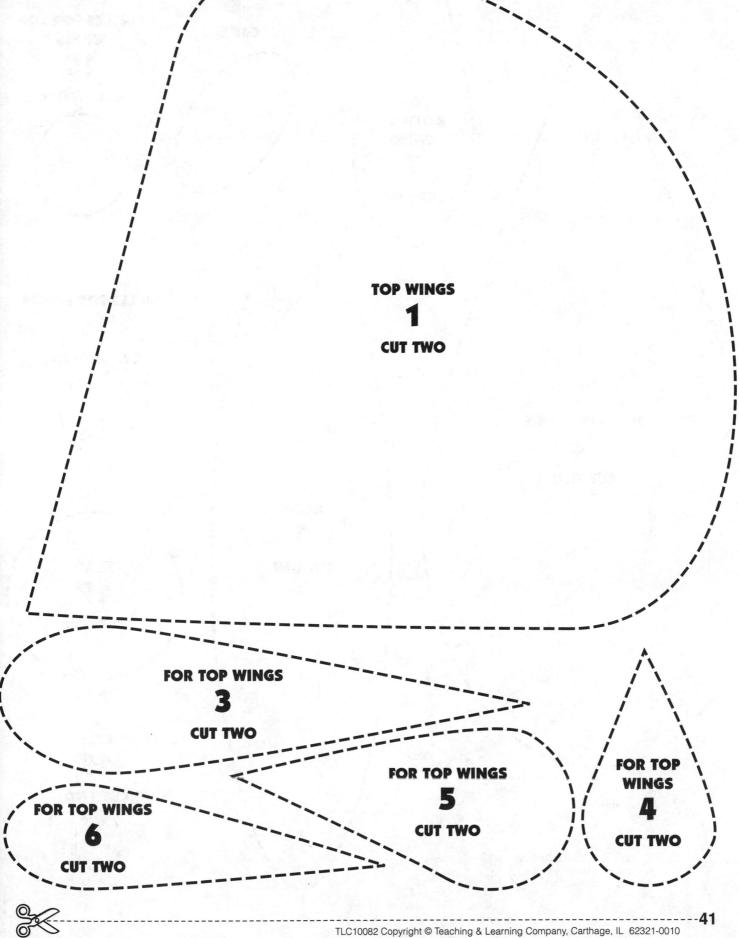

TOP WINGS
1
CUT TWO

FOR TOP WINGS
3
CUT TWO

FOR TOP WINGS
5
CUT TWO

FOR TOP
WINGS
4
CUT TWO

FOR TOP WINGS
6
CUT TWO

MONARCH BUTTERFLY PATTERNS

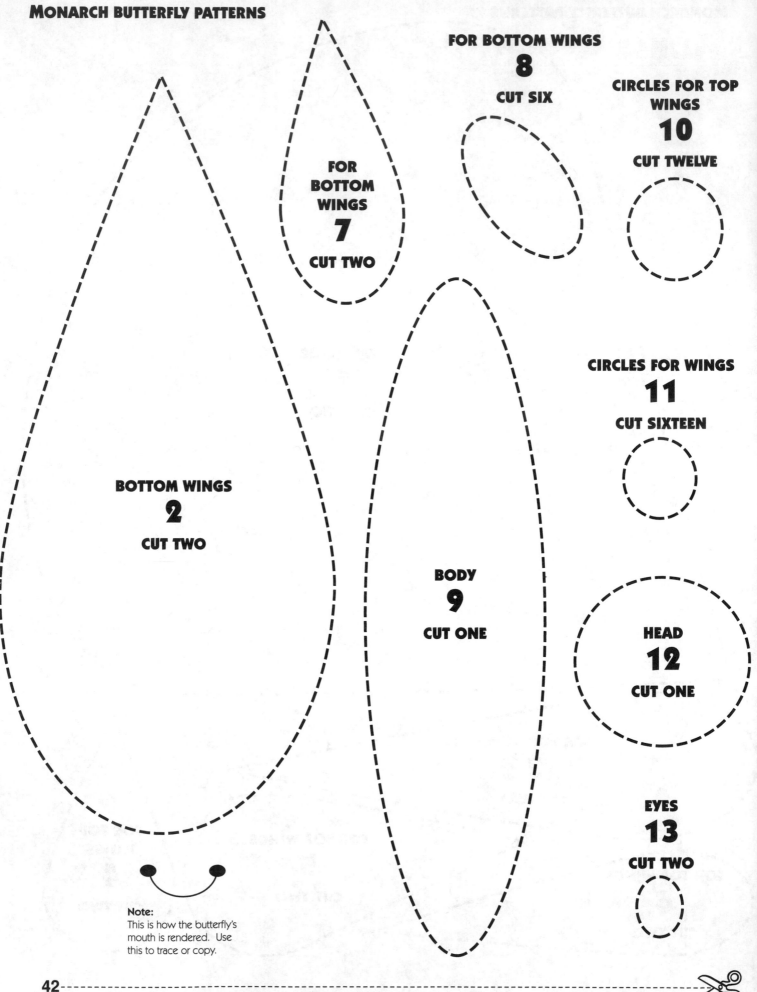

FOR BOTTOM WINGS
8
CUT SIX

CIRCLES FOR TOP WINGS
10
CUT TWELVE

FOR BOTTOM WINGS
7
CUT TWO

CIRCLES FOR WINGS
11
CUT SIXTEEN

BOTTOM WINGS
2
CUT TWO

BODY
9
CUT ONE

HEAD
12
CUT ONE

EYES
13
CUT TWO

Note:
This is how the butterfly's mouth is rendered. Use this to trace or copy.

Mouse

Materials: *black, gray, pink and white paper; scissors; glue; black crayon or marker*
Optional Materials: *gray yarn*

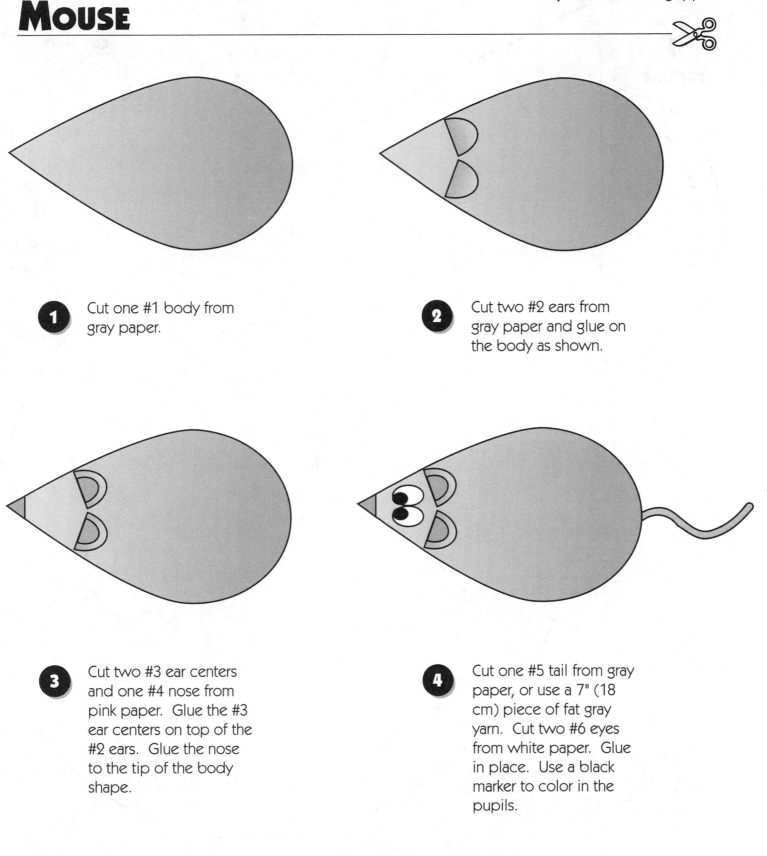

1 Cut one #1 body from gray paper.

2 Cut two #2 ears from gray paper and glue on the body as shown.

3 Cut two #3 ear centers and one #4 nose from pink paper. Glue the #3 ear centers on top of the #2 ears. Glue the nose to the tip of the body shape.

4 Cut one #5 tail from gray paper, or use a 7" (18 cm) piece of fat gray yarn. Cut two #6 eyes from white paper. Glue in place. Use a black marker to color in the pupils.

Note: Add a craft stick to the back and create a prop for "Hickory, Dickory, Dock" or other rhymes and stories.

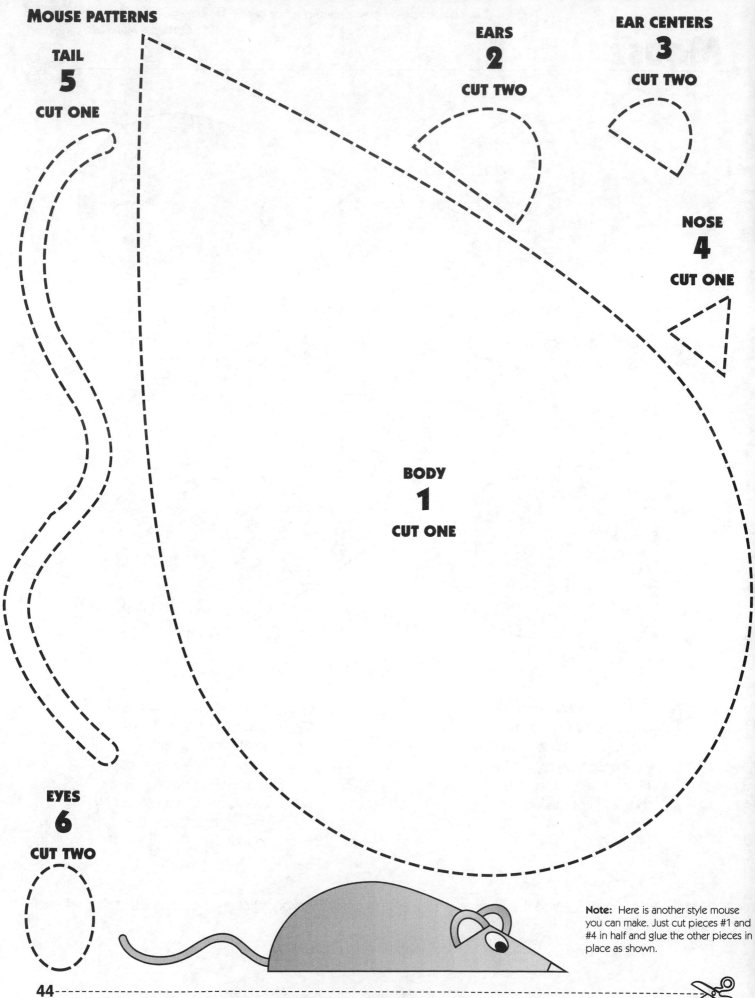

MOUSE PATTERNS

TAIL
5
CUT ONE

EARS
2
CUT TWO

EAR CENTERS
3
CUT TWO

NOSE
4
CUT ONE

BODY
1
CUT ONE

EYES
6
CUT TWO

Note: Here is another style mouse you can make. Just cut pieces #1 and #4 in half and glue the other pieces in place as shown.

Materials: *black, light and dark tan, white and yellow paper; scissors; glue; black crayon or marker*

POLYPHEMUS MOTH

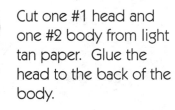

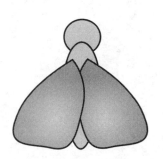

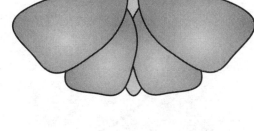

1 Cut one #1 head and one #2 body from light tan paper. Glue the head to the back of the body.

2 Cut two #3 bottom wings from dark tan paper. Glue the bottom wings together over the main body as shown.

3 Cut two #4 top wings from dark tan paper and glue to the top of the bottom wings as shown.

4 Cut two #5 bottom wing large circles from yellow paper and two #6 bottom wing small circles from black paper and glue to the bottom wings. Cut two #7 top wing ovals from yellow paper and two #8 top wing circles from black paper for the top wings. Glue in place as shown. (Note: If pieces #6 and #8 are too small for your students to cut out, color in the circle area with black crayon or marker.

5 Cut two #9 antennas from dark tan paper. Cut slits on either side of the triangle for a feathered-edge look. Cut two #10 eyes from white paper. Glue in place. Use a black marker to color in the pupils.

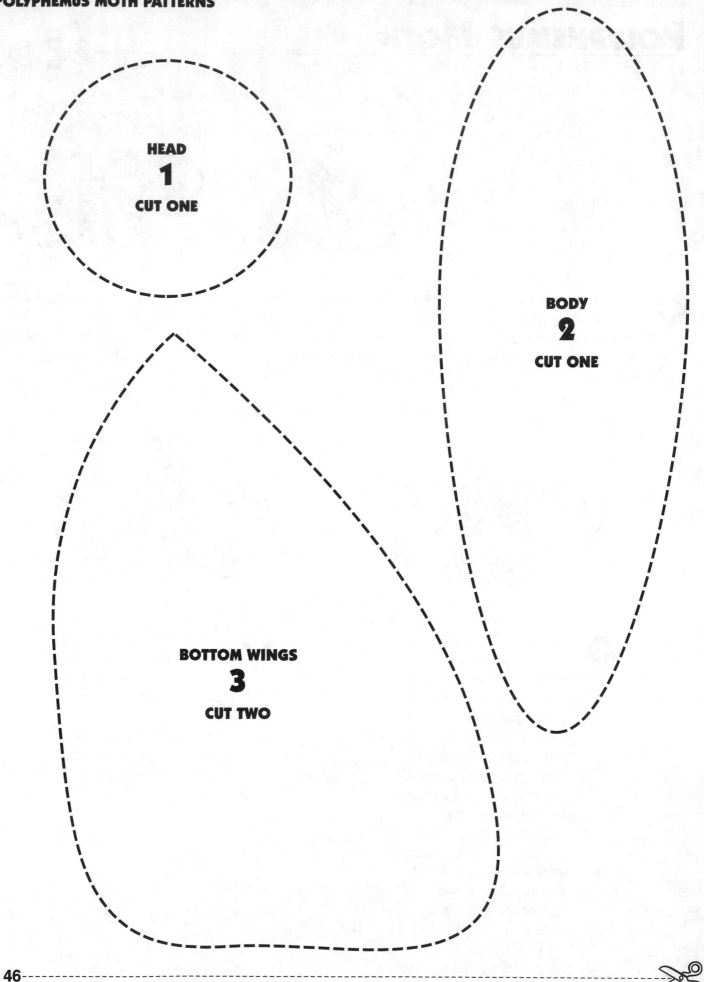

HEAD
1
CUT ONE

BODY
2
CUT ONE

BOTTOM WINGS
3
CUT TWO

POLYPHEMUS MOTH PATTERNS

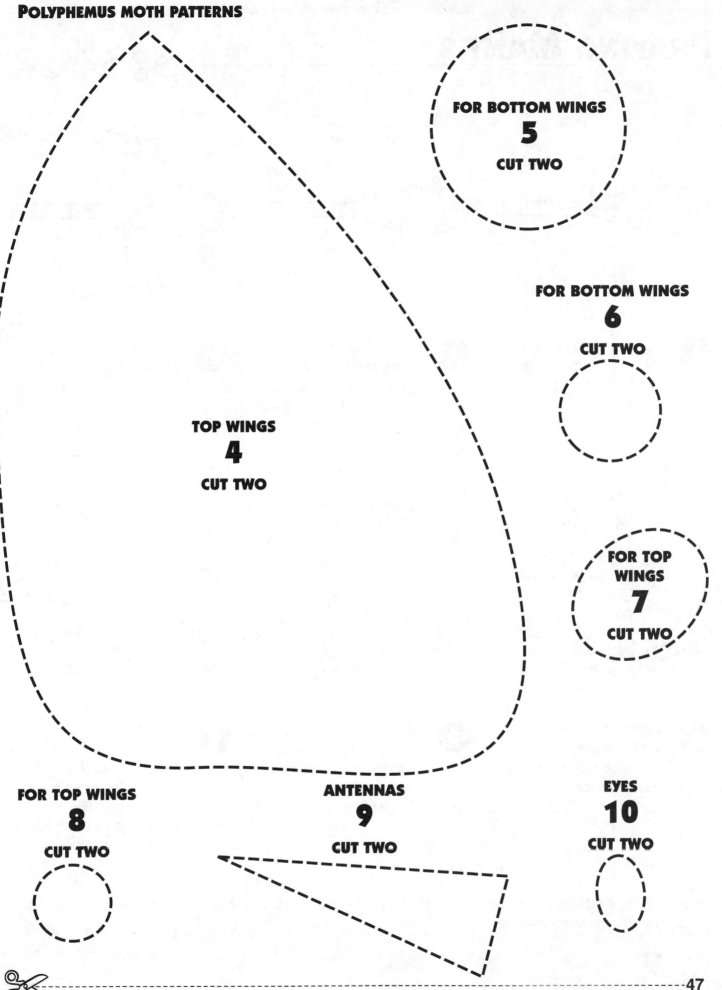

FOR BOTTOM WINGS
5
CUT TWO

FOR BOTTOM WINGS
6
CUT TWO

TOP WINGS
4
CUT TWO

FOR TOP WINGS
7
CUT TWO

FOR TOP WINGS
8
CUT TWO

ANTENNAS
9
CUT TWO

EYES
10
CUT TWO

Materials: black, mint green and white paper; scissors; glue; black crayon or marker

PRAYING MANTIS

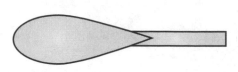

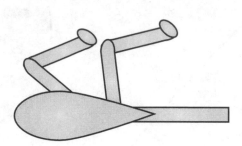

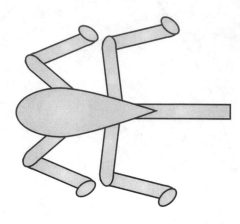

1   Cut one #1 tail and one #2 body from mint green paper. Glue together as shown.

2   Cut fourteen #3 legs and six #4 feet from mint green paper. Glue sets of back and side legs to the body as shown.

3   This is how the praying mantis should look now.

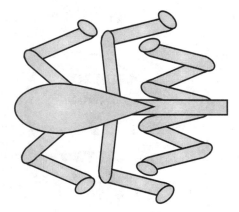

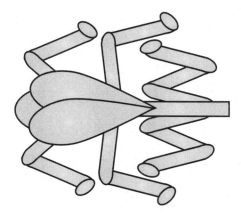

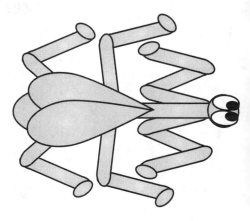

4   Zigzag the front legs to look as if they are praying. See illustration. Glue in place.

5   Cut two #5 wings from mint green paper and glue to the top of the body as shown. Overlap the wings.

6   Cut one #6 head from mint green paper and glue to the end of the body. Cut two #7 eyes from white paper. Glue in place. Use a black marker to color in the pupils.

Note: To make this easier for younger children, or beginners, have the back, side and front sets of legs and feet already glued together.

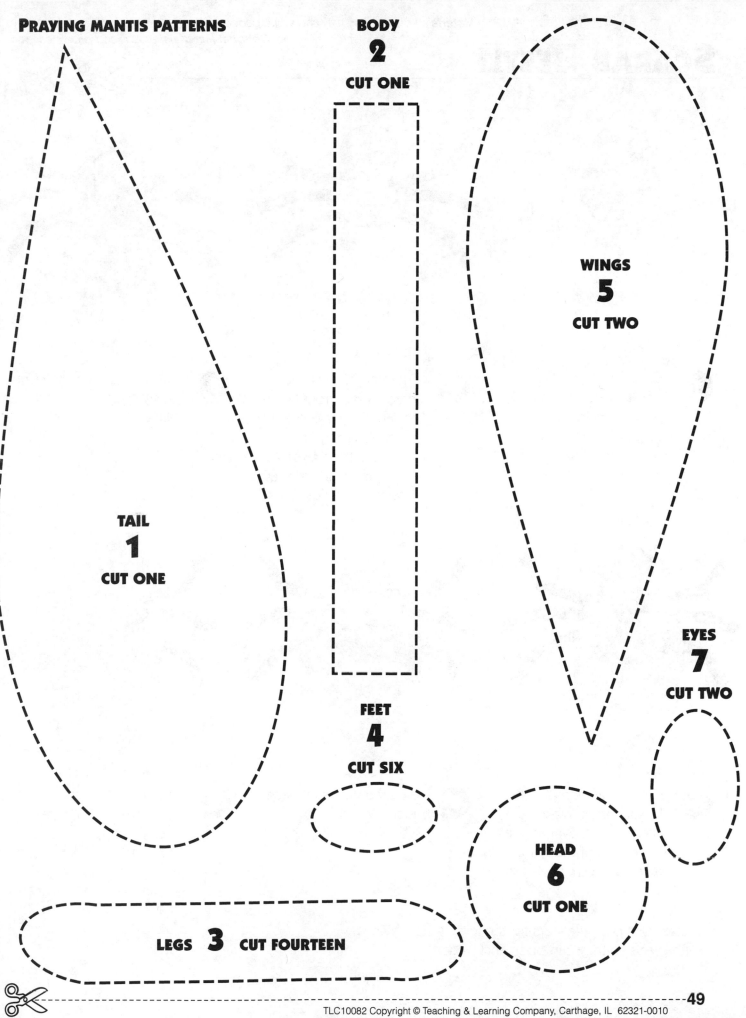

PRAYING MANTIS PATTERNS

BODY
2
CUT ONE

WINGS
5
CUT TWO

TAIL
1
CUT ONE

EYES
7
CUT TWO

FEET
4
CUT SIX

HEAD
6
CUT ONE

LEGS 3 CUT FOURTEEN

Materials: black, blue, gray and white paper; scissors; glue; black crayon or marker
Optional Materials: brads and pipe cleaners

SCARAB BEETLE

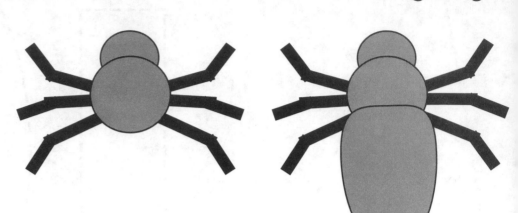

1 Cut one #1 head and one #2 body from dark gray paper and glue together as shown.

2 Cut three #3 legs and three #4 feet from black paper. Glue the #3 larger rectangles to the body. Then glue the #4 smaller rectangles to the legs as shown in the illustration.

3 Cut one #5 tail from dark gray paper and glue in place.

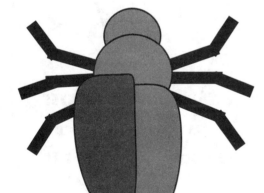

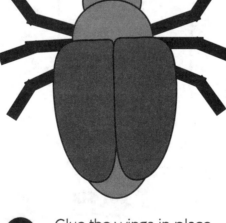

4 Cut two #6 wings from black paper. Make sure you flip one over so the flat edges of the wings face each other.

5 Glue the wings in place as shown.

6 Cut two #7 pinchers from black or gray paper and glue to the back of the head as shown. Cut two #8 eyes from black paper or use a marker to draw eyes on the head.

Note: Use pipe cleaners for the legs. Attach wings with brads so they can open and close.

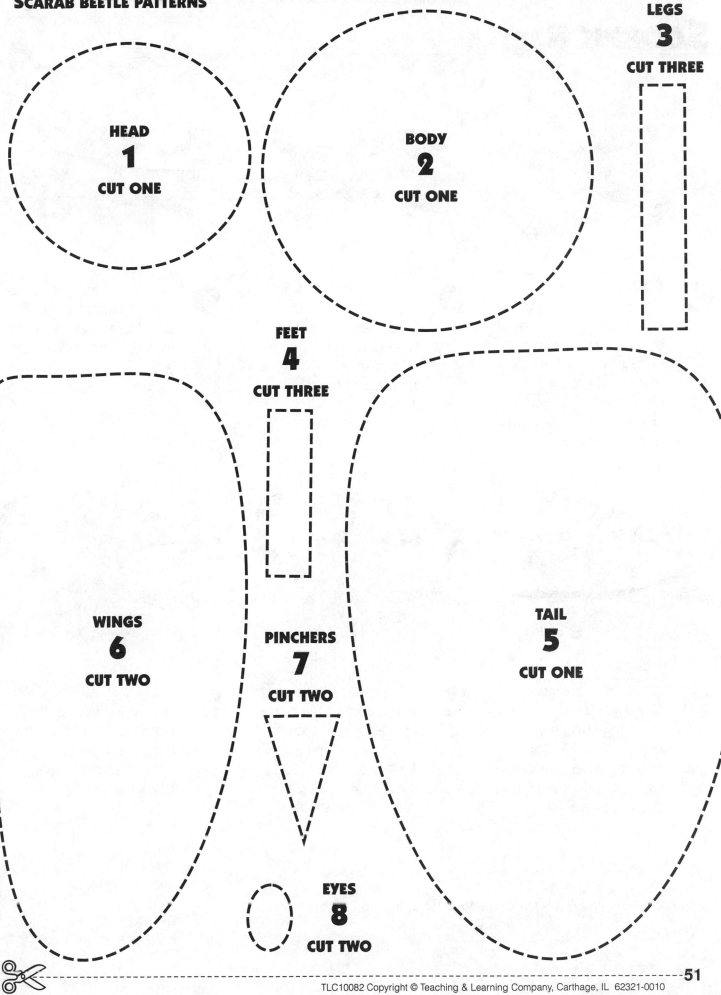

Scarab Beetle Patterns

HEAD
1
CUT ONE

BODY
2
CUT ONE

LEGS
3
CUT THREE

FEET
4
CUT THREE

WINGS
6
CUT TWO

PINCHERS
7
CUT TWO

TAIL
5
CUT ONE

EYES
8
CUT TWO

Materials: black and reddish brown paper, scissors, glue, black crayon or marker

SCORPION

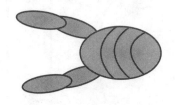

1 Cut one #1 body and four #2 front legs from reddish brown paper. Glue as shown. Draw on body section lines with black marker as illustrated. (Note: All of the body shapes will be cut from reddish brown paper.)

2 Cut two #3 top claws and three #4 claws. Glue one of #3 and one of #4 to form the pinchers and glue to #2. Save the extra #4 for the stinger.

3 Cut sixteen #5 legs. Glue two of each of these together as shown to form the inner part of the legs.

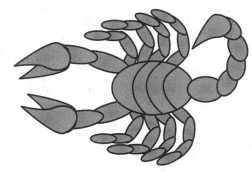

4 Cut sixteen #6 legs. Glue two of each of these together and attach to the #5 legs to form the outer part of the legs. (Note: Curve the legs forward.)

5 Cut one #7 tail and glue to the back of the body. Cut four #8 tail sections and glue forming a curve for the tail. Then glue the third #4 piece in place for the stinger.

6 Cut two #9 pinchers and glue to the front of the head. Cut two #10 eyes from black paper or color in pupils with a black marker.

Note: Preassemble legs for younger students or beginners.

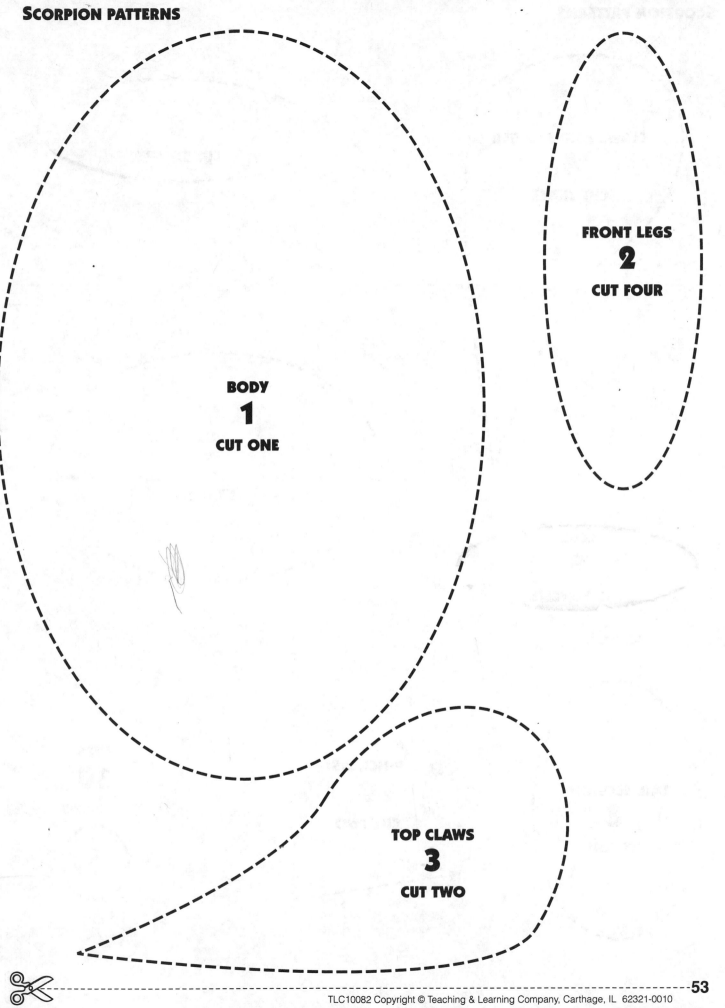

FRONT LEGS
2
CUT FOUR

BODY
1
CUT ONE

TOP CLAWS
3
CUT TWO

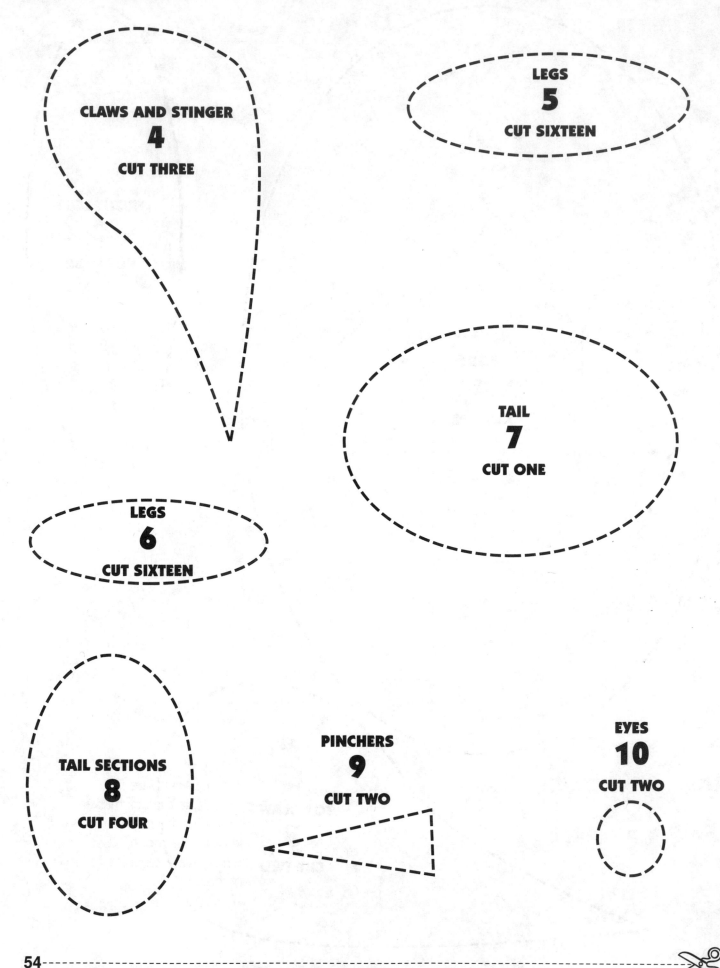

CLAWS AND STINGER
4
CUT THREE

LEGS
5
CUT SIXTEEN

LEGS
6
CUT SIXTEEN

TAIL
7
CUT ONE

TAIL SECTIONS
8
CUT FOUR

PINCHERS
9
CUT TWO

EYES
10
CUT TWO

Materials: *black, four shades of pink or peach, light green and white paper; scissors; glue; black crayon or marker; pipe cleaners*

SNAIL

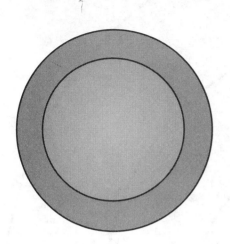 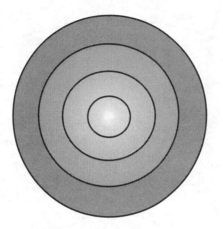 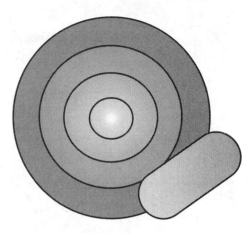

1 Cut one each of the #1 body circles from four different shades of pink or peach paper. It is best to start with the largest circle in the darkest shade and work to the lightest.

2 This is the how to glue the circles together.

3 Cut one #2 body from light green paper. Glue at the right side of the circles as shown.

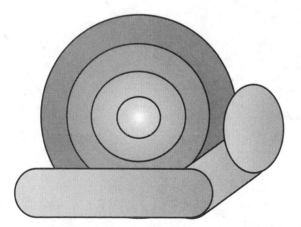 

4 Cut one #3 head from light green paper and glue to the body. Cut one #4 bottom body from light green paper and glue to the bottom of the circles as shown.

5 Cut two #5 eyes from white paper. Glue in place. Use a black marker to color in the pupils and draw on the mouth. Use chenille pipe cleaners for antennas.

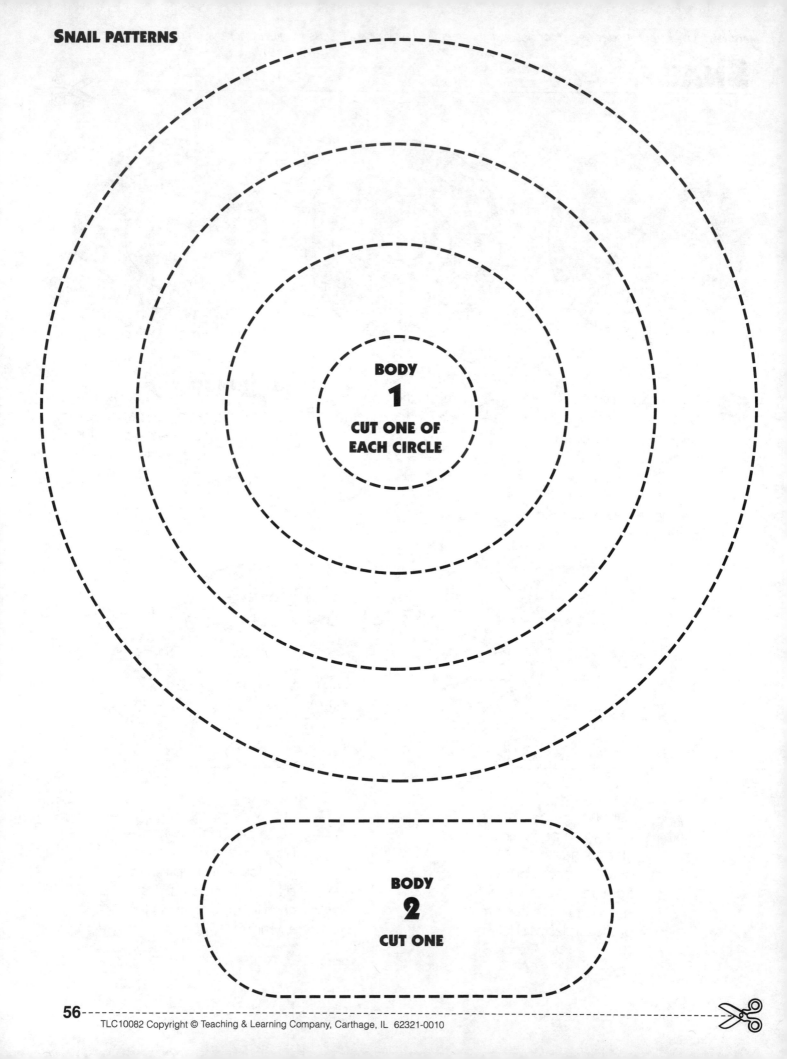

BODY
1
CUT ONE OF
EACH CIRCLE

BODY
2
CUT ONE

SNAIL PATTERNS

Snail Mail: Glue finished snails to manila envelopes. Use to communicate with students or to send home.

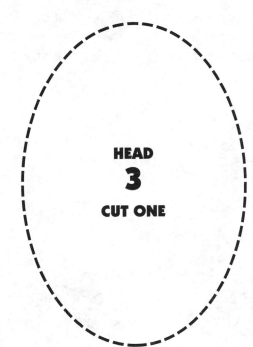

HEAD
3
CUT ONE

BOTTOM BODY
4
CUT ONE

EYES
5

CUT TWO

Note:
This is how the snail's mouth is rendered. Use this to trace or copy.

Materials: *black, mint green and white paper; scissors; glue; black crayon or marker; pipe cleaners*

SWALLOWTAIL BUTTERFLY

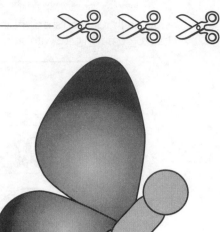

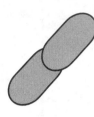

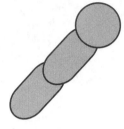

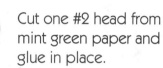

1 Cut two #1 body pieces from mint green and glue to form the body as shown.

2 Cut one #2 head from mint green paper and glue in place.

3 Cut one #3 top wing and one #4 bottom wing from black paper and glue as shown.

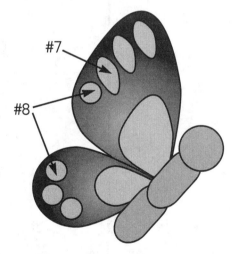

#7

#8

4 Cut one #5 top wing inset and one #6 bottom wing inset and glue onto the wings as shown. Cut three #7 shapes and four #8 circles for the outer edges of the wings. Glue in place as shown.

5 Cut six #9 legs from mint green paper. Glue two #9 legs together at a slight angle to form three sets of legs. Glue the legs onto the body. Cut three #10 feet from mint green paper and glue to the ends of the legs.

6 Cut one #11 tail and four #12 scallops to form the swallowtail. Glue as shown. Cut two #13 eyes from white paper. Glue in place. Color in the pupils with a black marker and draw on the mouth. Add chenille pipe cleaners for antennas.

Note: Preassemble the legs and feet for younger students or beginners.

Swallowtail Butterfly Patterns

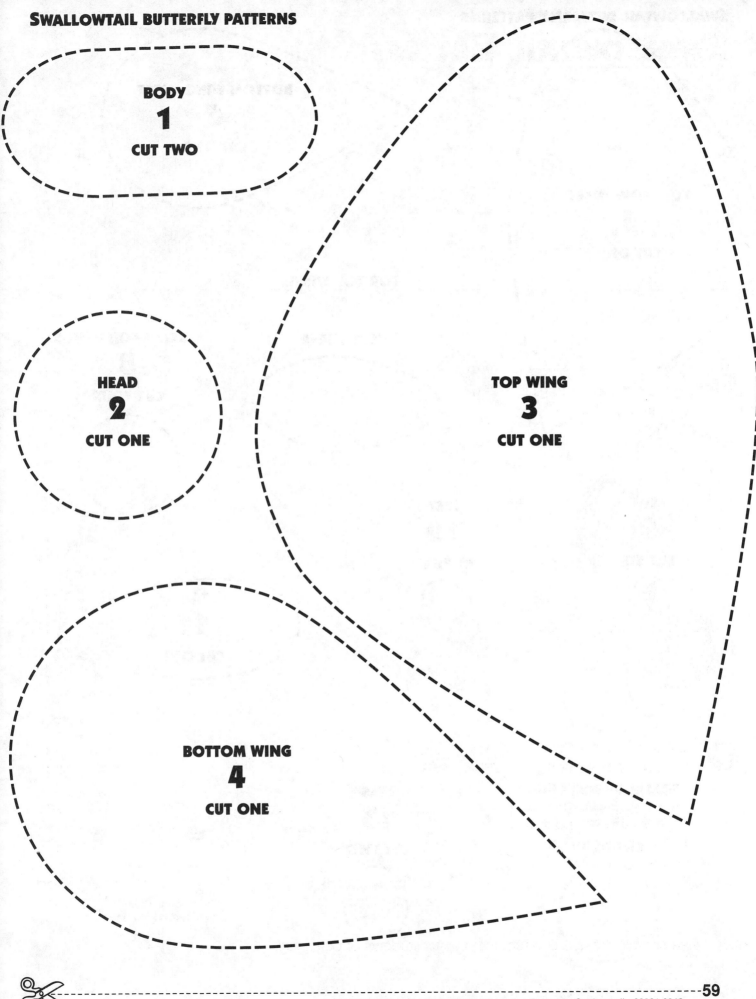

BODY
1
CUT TWO

HEAD
2
CUT ONE

TOP WING
3
CUT ONE

BOTTOM WING
4
CUT ONE

SWALLOWTAIL BUTTERFLY PATTERNS

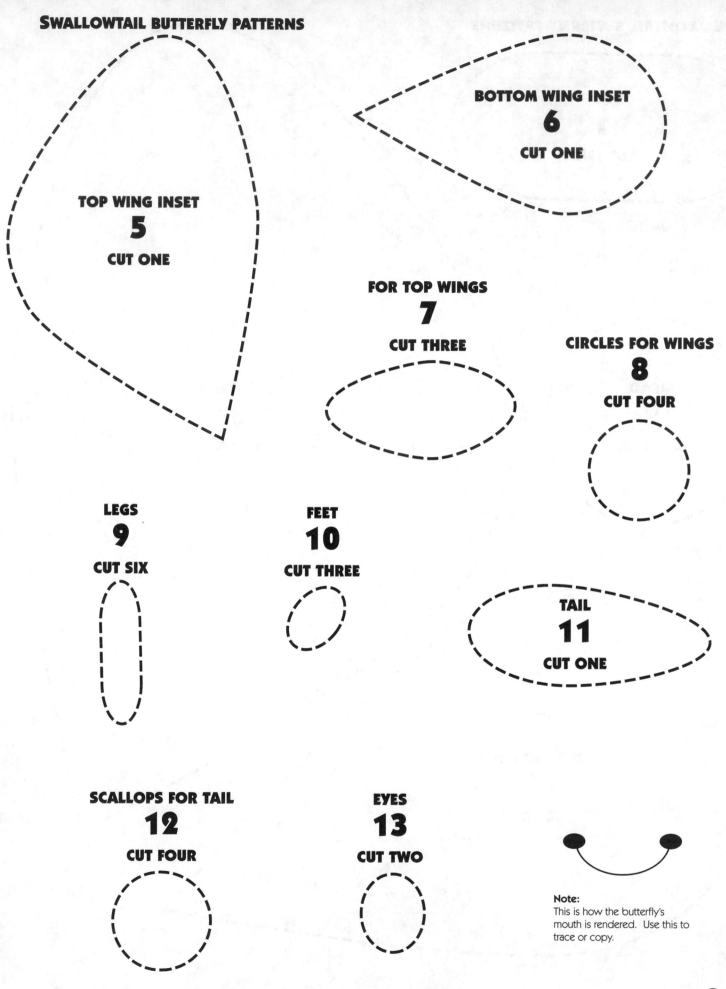

TOP WING INSET
5
CUT ONE

BOTTOM WING INSET
6
CUT ONE

FOR TOP WINGS
7
CUT THREE

CIRCLES FOR WINGS
8
CUT FOUR

LEGS
9
CUT SIX

FEET
10
CUT THREE

TAIL
11
CUT ONE

SCALLOPS FOR TAIL
12
CUT FOUR

EYES
13
CUT TWO

Note:
This is how the butterfly's
mouth is rendered. Use this to
trace or copy.

Materials: *black, green and white paper; scissors; glue; black crayon or marker*

TADPOLE

1 Cut one #1 body and one #2 tail from green paper. Glue together as shown. Stop here for tadpole. Add one #6 eye. Continue for tadpole/frog figure.

2 Cut three #3 legs from green paper. Glue as shown.

3 Cut six #4 toes and two #5 feet from green paper. Glue three #4 toes on the end of each #3 leg and then finish by gluing a #5 foot on top of each set of toes.

4 Cut one #6 eye from white paper and glue as shown. Color in the pupil and draw on a mouth with a black crayon or marker.

Note: Make the tadpole out of green felt and use as a bookmark, or use the tadpoles with the cattail on page 78 for an attractive bulletin board.

TADPOLE PATTERNS

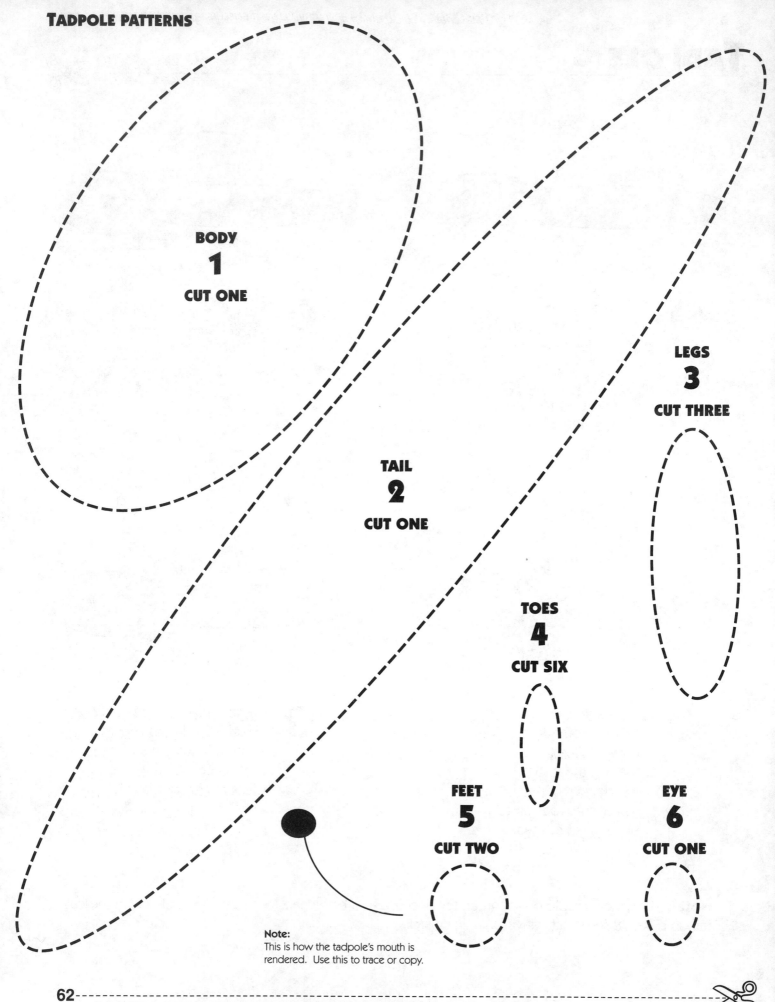

BODY
1
CUT ONE

TAIL
2
CUT ONE

LEGS
3
CUT THREE

TOES
4
CUT SIX

FEET
5
CUT TWO

EYE
6
CUT ONE

Note:
This is how the tadpole's mouth is rendered. Use this to trace or copy.

TREE FROG

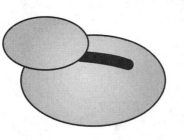

#4

#4

#5

1 Cut one #1 body from bright green paper. Cut one #2 stripe from black paper and glue as shown. Stripe can be drawn on with a crayon or marker.

2 Cut one #3 head from bright green paper and glue in place.

3 Cut two #4 legs and one #5 leg from bright green paper. Glue the smaller #4 leg on first, then the larger #5 leg, then the smaller #4 leg as shown.

4 Cut two #6 front legs from bright green paper. Glue in place as shown. Cut nine #7 toes from bright green paper. Glue three toes to the back leg and three toes to each of the front legs as illustrated.

5 Cut two #8 feet from bright green paper and glue over the front toe and leg parts as shown.

6 Cut two #9 eyes from bright green paper and glue in place. Cut two #10 eyes from white paper. Glue in place. Color in the pupils and draw on a mouth with a black marker.

Note: *Preassemble legs and feet for younger students or beginners.*

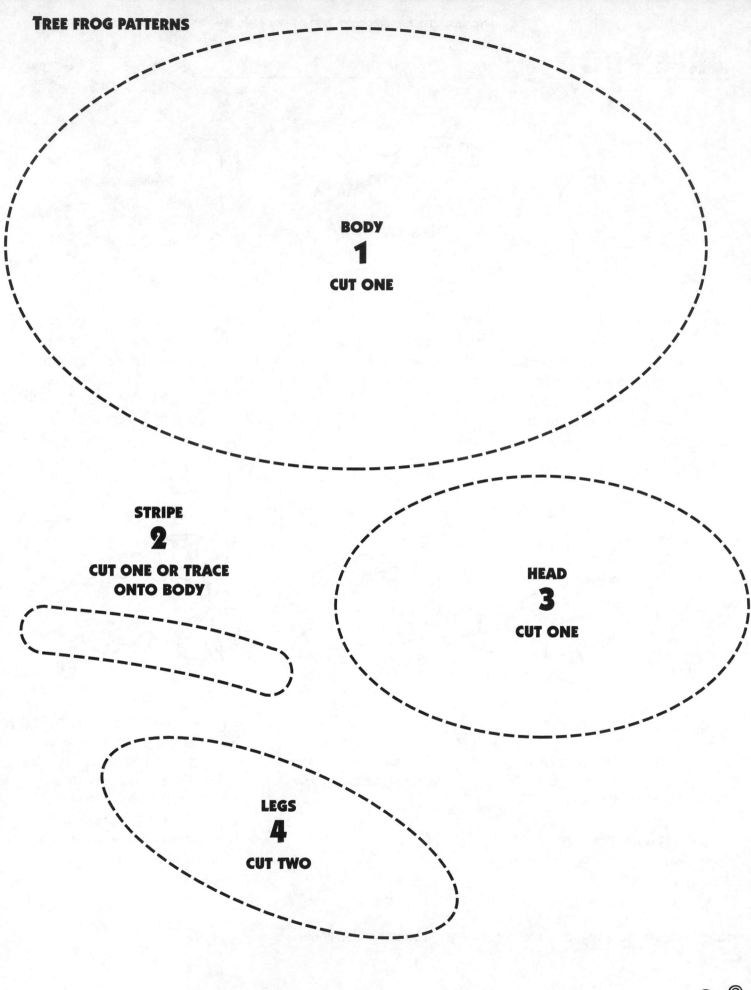

BODY
1
CUT ONE

STRIPE
2
CUT ONE OR TRACE
ONTO BODY

HEAD
3
CUT ONE

LEGS
4
CUT TWO

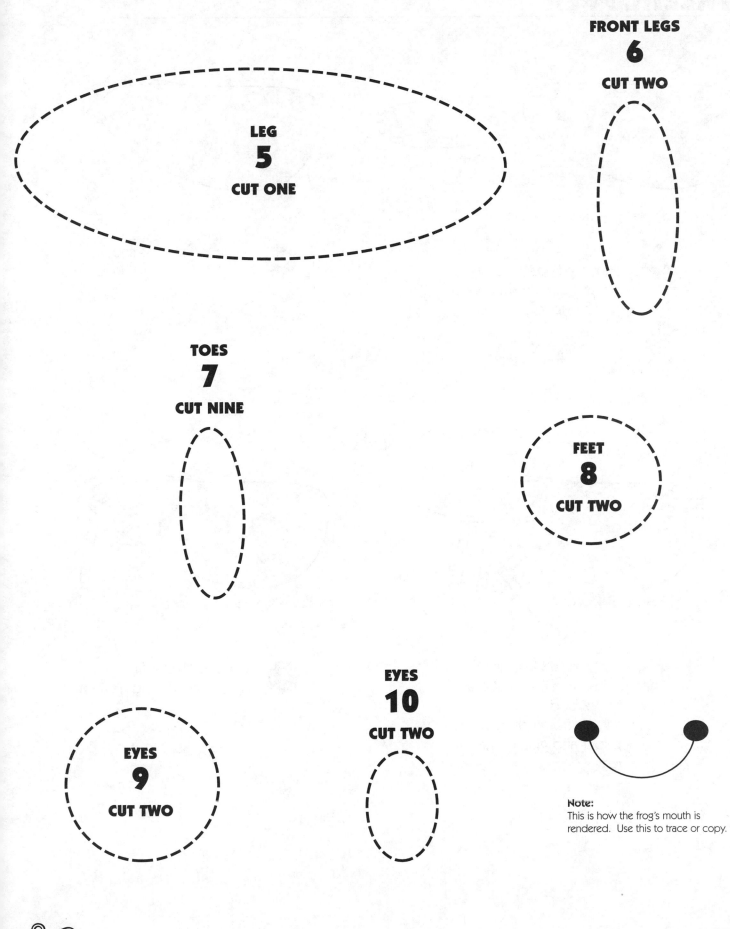

FRONT LEGS
6
CUT TWO

LEG
5
CUT ONE

TOES
7
CUT NINE

FEET
8
CUT TWO

EYES
10
CUT TWO

EYES
9
CUT TWO

Note:
This is how the frog's mouth is
rendered. Use this to trace or copy.

TREEHOPPER

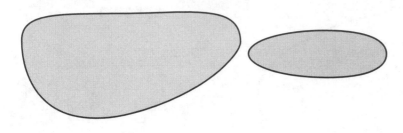

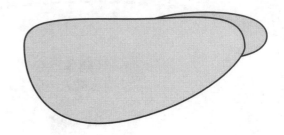

1   Cut one #1 wing from light green paper and one #2 body from dark green paper.

2   Glue together as shown.

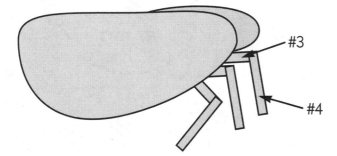

#3

#4

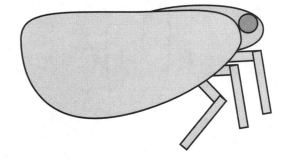

3   Cut three #3 legs from light green paper. Glue to the body. Cut three #4 feet from light green paper and glue to the legs.

4   Cut one #5 eye from orange paper and glue in place.

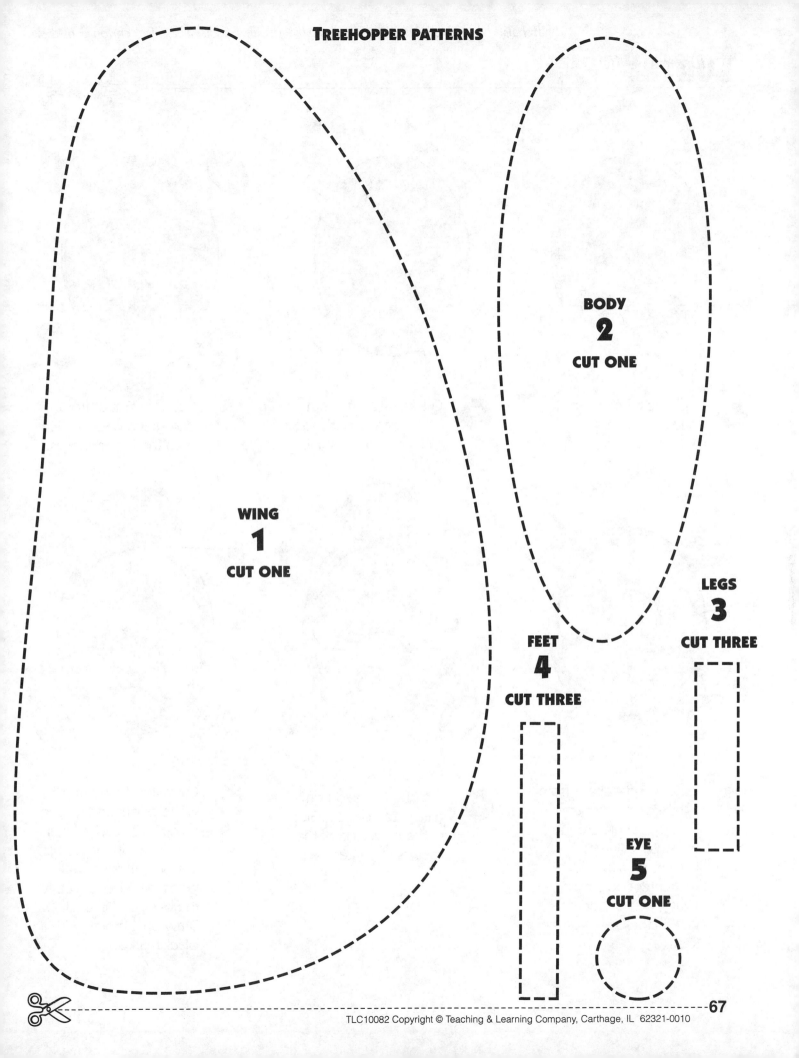

TREEHOPPER PATTERNS

BODY
2
CUT ONE

WING
1
CUT ONE

LEGS
3
CUT THREE

FEET
4
CUT THREE

EYE
5
CUT ONE

Materials: *black, two shades of green and white paper; scissors; glue; black crayon or marker*

TURTLE

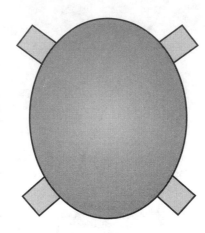

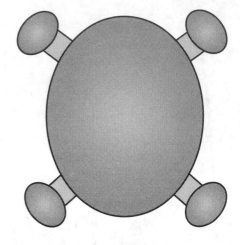

1 Cut one #1 shell from dark green paper.

2 Cut four #2 legs from light green paper and glue around the shell.

3 Cut four #3 feet from dark green paper. Glue onto the leg as shown.

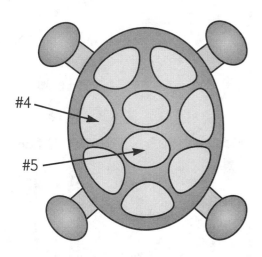

#4 —→

#5 —→

4 Cut seven #4 spots from light green paper and glue in a circle around the outer edge of the shell as shown. Cut two #5 center spots from light green paper and glue in the center of the shell.

5 Cut one #6 head from dark green paper. Glue to the back side of the shell as illustrated.

6 Cut two #7 eyes from white paper and glue in place. Use a black marker to color in the pupils. Cut one #8 tail from light green paper and glue to the base of the shell. Draw on a mouth with a black marker.

SHELL

1

CUT ONE

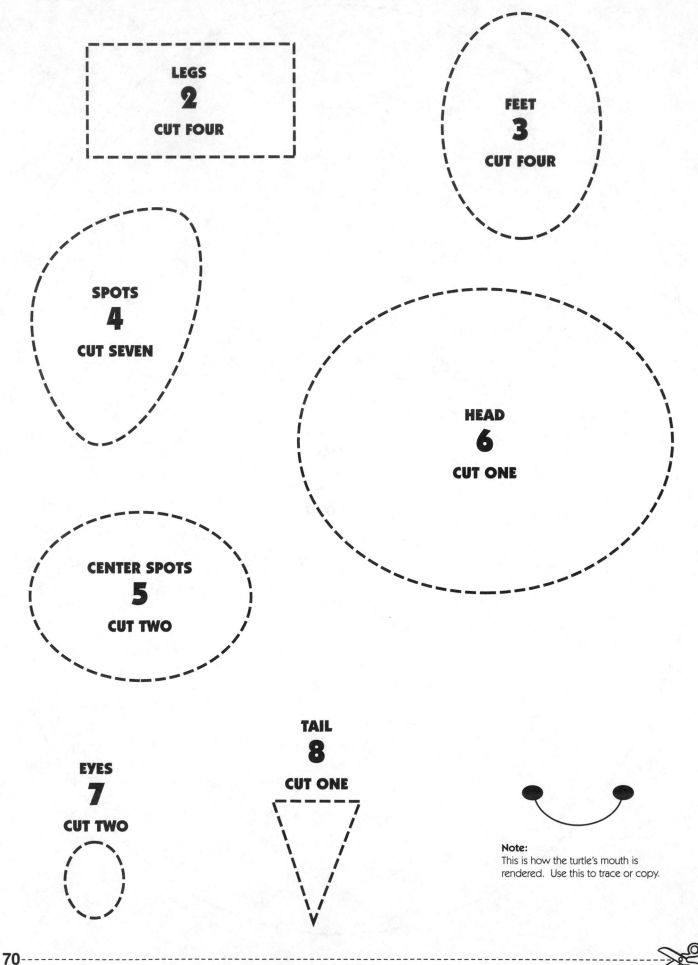

LEGS
2
CUT FOUR

FEET
3
CUT FOUR

SPOTS
4
CUT SEVEN

HEAD
6
CUT ONE

CENTER SPOTS
5
CUT TWO

EYES
7
CUT TWO

TAIL
8
CUT ONE

Note:
This is how the turtle's mouth is rendered. Use this to trace or copy.

Materials: black, dark gray and white paper, scissors, glue, black crayon or marker, pipe cleaners

WASP

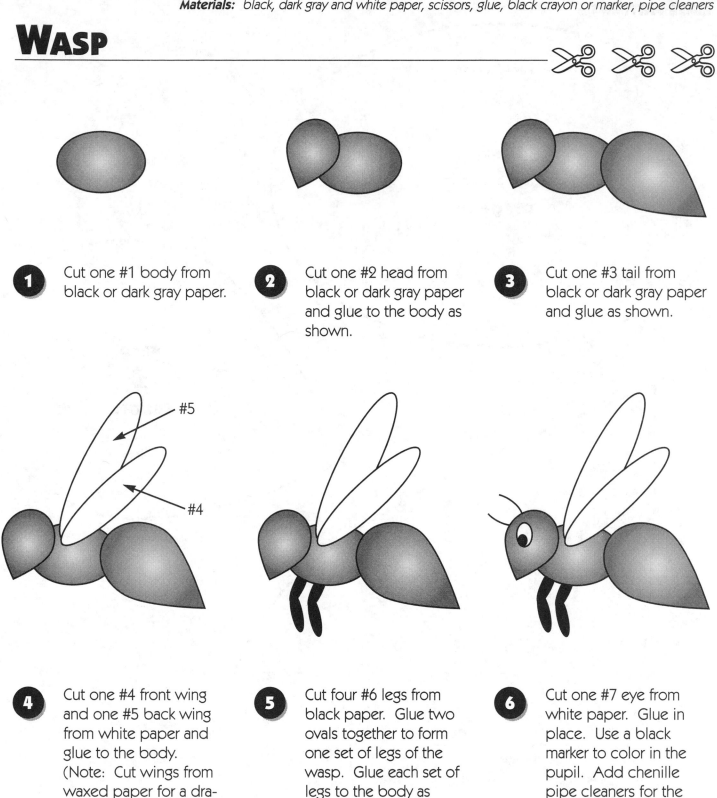

1 Cut one #1 body from black or dark gray paper.

2 Cut one #2 head from black or dark gray paper and glue to the body as shown.

3 Cut one #3 tail from black or dark gray paper and glue as shown.

4 Cut one #4 front wing and one #5 back wing from white paper and glue to the body. (Note: Cut wings from waxed paper for a dramatic effect.)

5 Cut four #6 legs from black paper. Glue two ovals together to form one set of legs of the wasp. Glue each set of legs to the body as shown.

6 Cut one #7 eye from white paper. Glue in place. Use a black marker to color in the pupil. Add chenille pipe cleaners for the antennas.

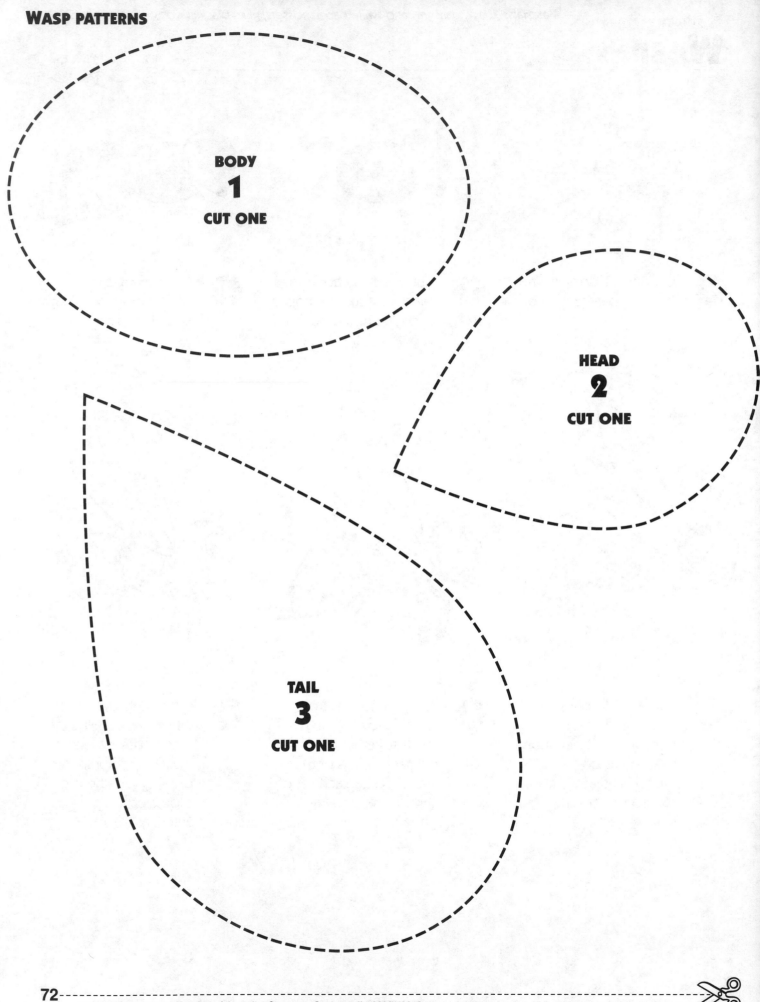

BODY
1
CUT ONE

HEAD
2
CUT ONE

TAIL
3
CUT ONE

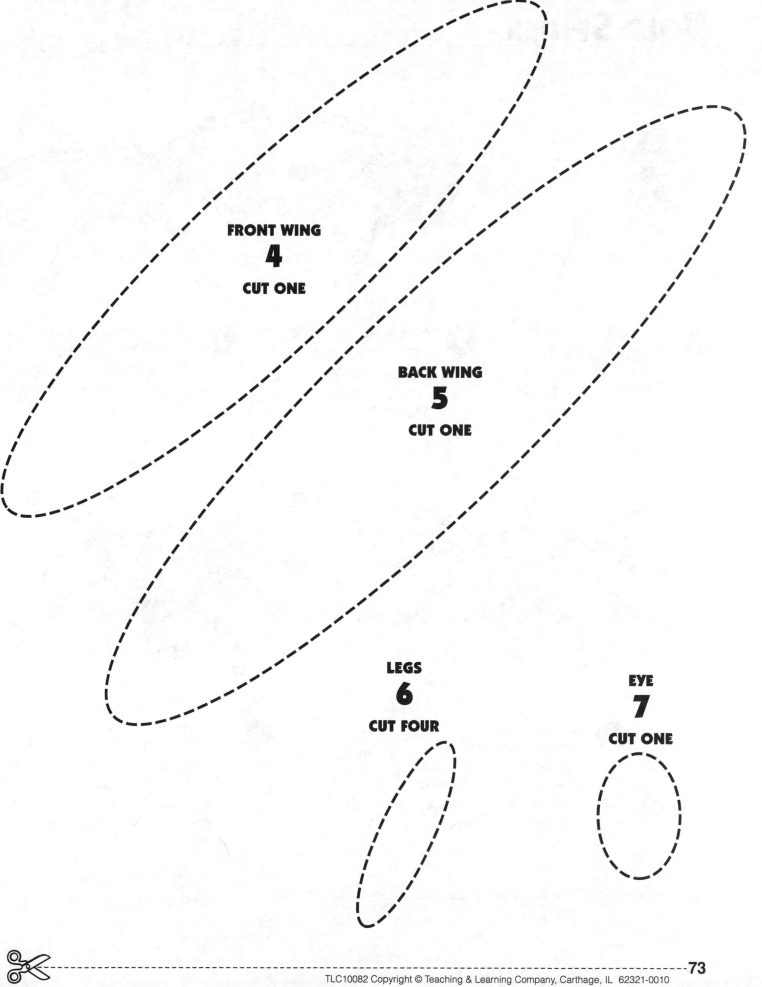

FRONT WING
4
CUT ONE

BACK WING
5
CUT ONE

LEGS
6
CUT FOUR

EYE
7
CUT ONE

Materials: *black, brown, tan and white paper; scissors; glue; black crayon or marker*

WOLF SPIDER

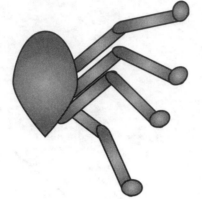

1 Cut one #1 body from brown paper. Cut sixteen #2 legs and eight #3 feet from brown paper.

2 Start gluing four #2 leg sections to each side of the main body as shown. Then glue a second leg section to each leg.

3 Finally, glue a #3 foot to each of the eight legs. This is how your spider should look now.

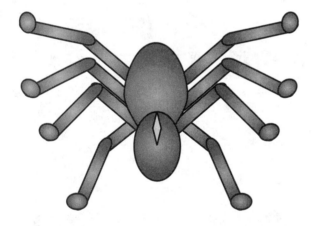

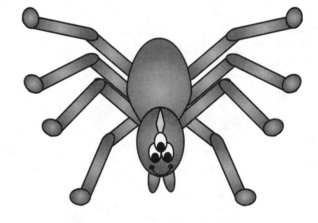

4 Cut one #4 head from brown paper and glue on the body. Cut one #5 diamond from tan paper and glue at the back of the head as shown.

5 Cut one #6 eyes from white paper and use a black marker to color in the pupils. (Spiders have more than two eyes.) Glue in place. Cut two #7 fangs and glue as shown. Draw on a mouth with a black marker.

Note: Preassemble legs for younger students or beginners.

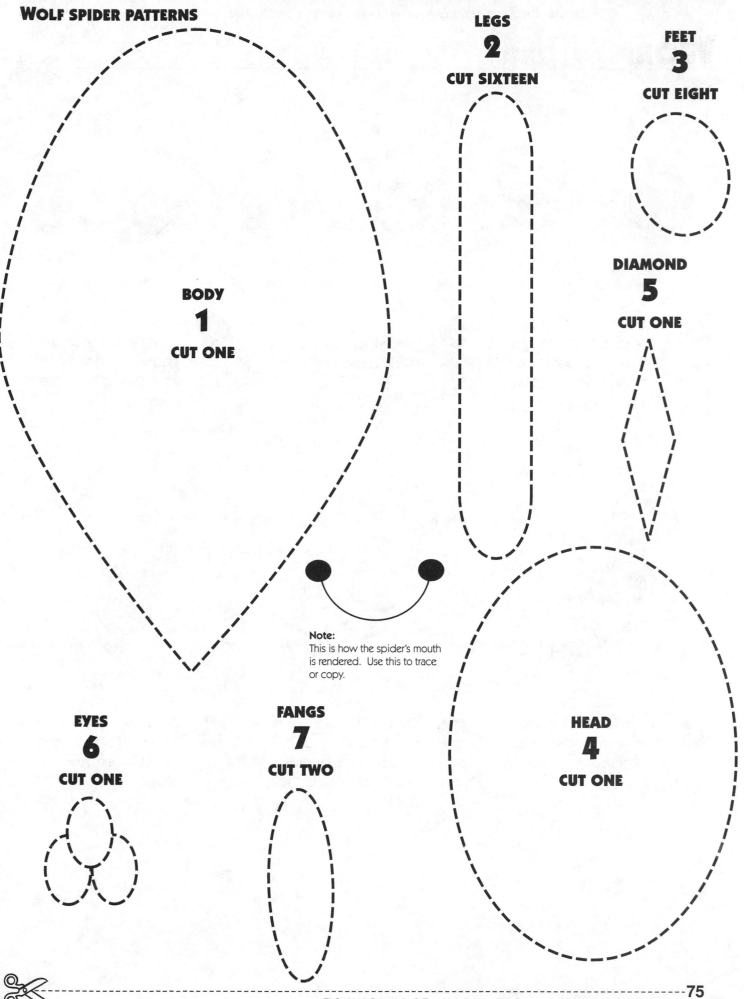

WOLF SPIDER PATTERNS

BODY
1
CUT ONE

LEGS
2
CUT SIXTEEN

FEET
3
CUT EIGHT

DIAMOND
5
CUT ONE

Note:
This is how the spider's mouth is rendered. Use this to trace or copy.

EYES
6
CUT ONE

FANGS
7
CUT TWO

HEAD
4
CUT ONE

Materials: black, pale pink or green and white paper; scissors; glue; black crayon or marker; pipe cleaners

WORM

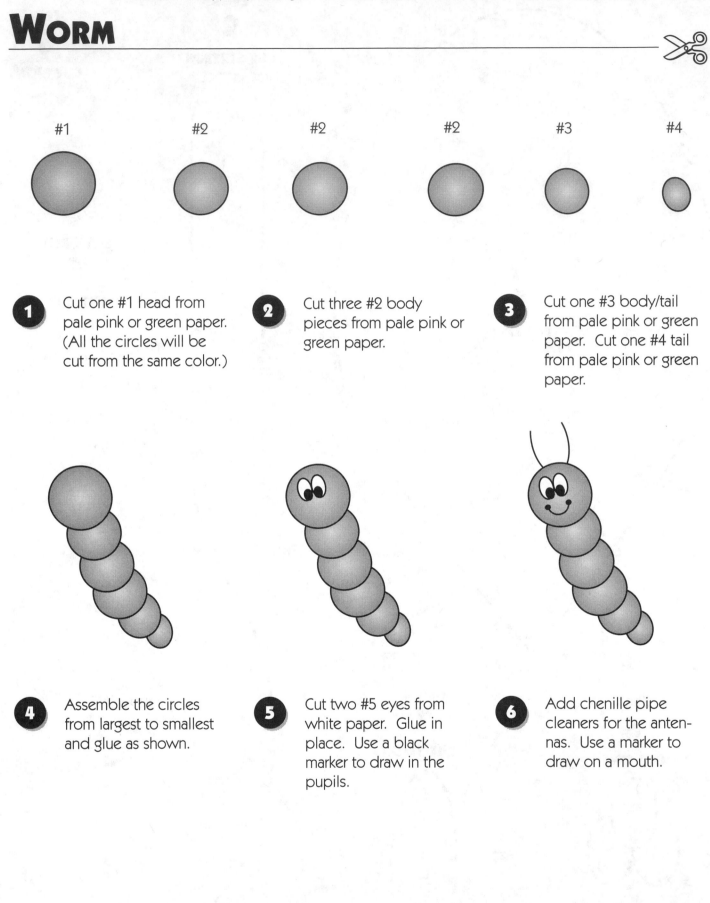

#1 #2 #2 #2 #3 #4

1 Cut one #1 head from pale pink or green paper. (All the circles will be cut from the same color.)

2 Cut three #2 body pieces from pale pink or green paper.

3 Cut one #3 body/tail from pale pink or green paper. Cut one #4 tail from pale pink or green paper.

4 Assemble the circles from largest to smallest and glue as shown.

5 Cut two #5 eyes from white paper. Glue in place. Use a black marker to draw in the pupils.

6 Add chenille pipe cleaners for the antennas. Use a marker to draw on a mouth.

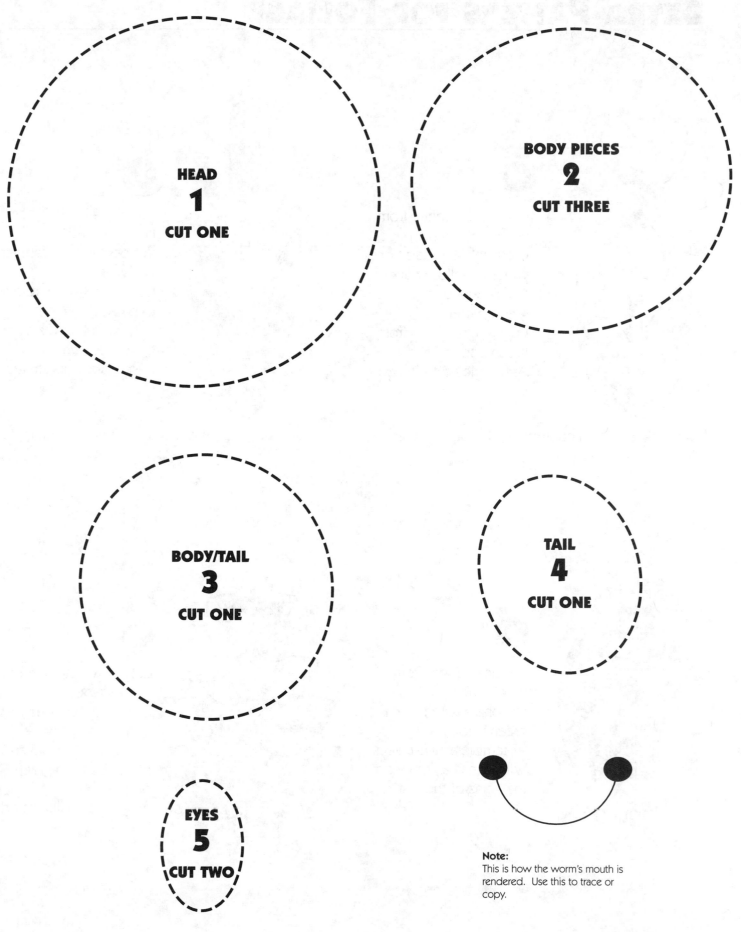

HEAD
1
CUT ONE

BODY PIECES
2
CUT THREE

BODY/TAIL
3
CUT ONE

TAIL
4
CUT ONE

EYES
5
CUT TWO

Note:
This is how the worm's mouth is
rendered. Use this to trace or
copy.

Materials: *brown, green, orange, tan, white and yellow paper; scissors; glue; black crayon or marker*

EXTRA PATTERS FOR FOLIAGE

1

Cut one #1 center from yellow or orange paper.
Cut eight #2 petals from white or yellow paper.
Cut one #3 stem from green paper.
Cut two #4 leaves from green paper.
Assemble as illustrated.

Note: Flower petals cut from wallpaper samples make an interesting display.

2

Cut one #1 cattail from brown paper.
Cut one #2 top from tan paper.
Cut one #3 stem from tan paper.
Cut two #4 leaves from green paper.
Assemble as illustrated.

Note: Use felt or flocked paper for the cattail.

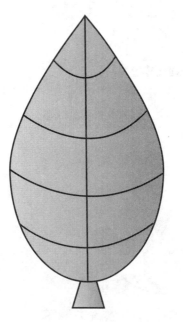

3

Cut one #1 leaf from green paper.
Cut one #2 stem from green paper.
Assemble as illustrated. With a marker, draw on the veins of the leaf as shown.

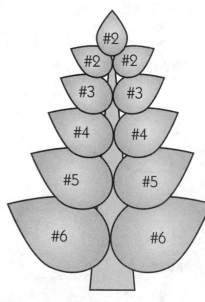

4

Cut one #1 stem from green paper.
Cut three #2 top leaves from green paper.
Cut two #3, #4, #5 and #6 leaves from green paper.
Assemble as illustrated.

1 FLOWER ———————————————————————

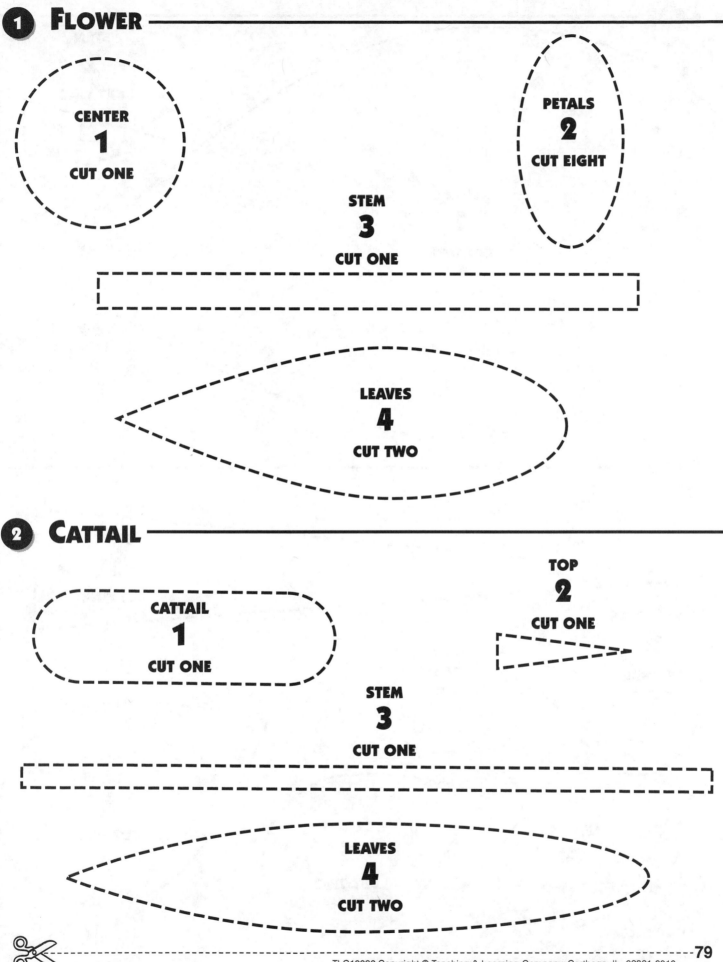

CENTER
1
CUT ONE

PETALS
2
CUT EIGHT

STEM
3
CUT ONE

LEAVES
4
CUT TWO

2 CATTAIL ———————————————————————

CATTAIL
1
CUT ONE

TOP
2
CUT ONE

STEM
3
CUT ONE

LEAVES
4
CUT TWO

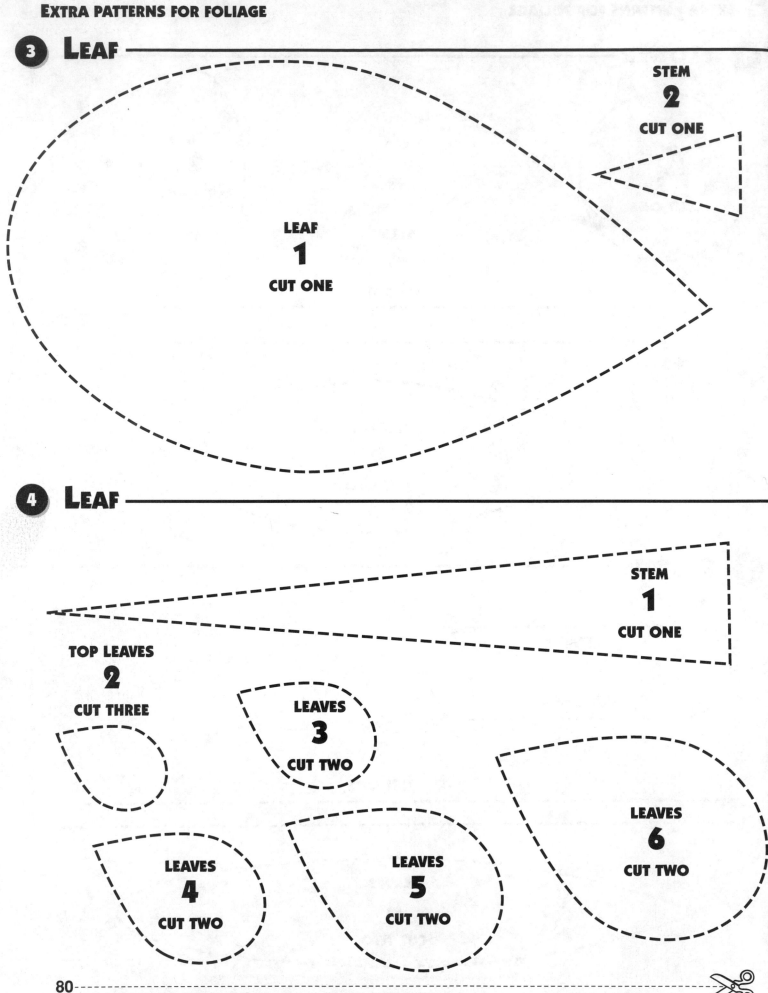

3 **LEAF**

STEM
2
CUT ONE

LEAF
1
CUT ONE

4 **LEAF**

STEM
1
CUT ONE

TOP LEAVES
2
CUT THREE

LEAVES
3
CUT TWO

LEAVES
4
CUT TWO

LEAVES
5
CUT TWO

LEAVES
6
CUT TWO